100 Years at Mackinac

A Centennial History of the Mackinac Island
State Park Commission 1895-1995

by David A. Armour

David A. Armour, Deputy Director, Mackinac Island State Park Commission, has served in that capacity since 1967.

A native of Grove City, Pennsylvania, he is a graduate of Calvin College (B.A. 1959) and Northwestern University (M.A. 1960 and Ph.D., 1965). While teaching at the University of Wisconsin-Milwaukee he came to work at Mackinac during the summers of 1965 and 1966. Author of numerous books and articles, he has shared Mackinac with his wife, Grace, and their four children, Marian, Arthur, David, and Anneke, who grew up and worked on Mackinac Island.

100 Years at Mackinac
A Centennial History of the Mackinac Island
State Park Commission 1895-1995

by David A. Armour

Mackinac State Historic Parks,
Mackinac Island, Michigan
© 1995 Mackinac State Historic Parks

ISBN 911872-63-9

First Edition

First Printing 5,000 copies

Editor: Graydon DeCamp

Art Director: Thomas Kachadurian

COMMISSIONERS - 1895

George T. Arnold

William M. Clark
Secretary

Thomas W. Ferry
President

Albert M. Stephens
Treasurer

Peter White
Vice President

COMMISSIONERS - 1995

L. Margaret Brown
Vice Chairperson

Dennis O. Cawthorne
Chairman

Richard P. Kughn

Kenneth C. Teysen
Secretary

Stephen Vogel

Erica A. Ward

Charles W. Yob

EDISON SAULT

CELEBRATING THE 100th ANNIVERSARY of Mackinac Island State Park and the Mackinac Island State Park Commission provides Edison Sault Electric Company with a special opportunity to bring together two forces which are at the heart of our northern Michigan area. Electric power ties together the many communities we serve in the eastern Upper Peninsula, and Mackinac Island is the world-renowned gem of our beautiful region.

As an investor-owned utility serving 22,000 customers from Mackinac in the east, to Sault Ste. Marie in the north, and as far as Fayette State Park in the Garden Peninsula in the west, we are aware of the many benefits brought to Michigan and the UP through the preservation of Mackinac Island State Park. Since the mid-19th century, travelers have come to enjoy the scenic beauty, natural wonders, and historic sites of what was America's second national park and Michigan's first state park. These visitors helped us to build a system of parks and museums and a vibrant economy from which we all benefit.

From the earliest days of Mackinac Island State Park, the Park Commission has been involved with the provision of electric power to the island. Edison Sault Electric Company and Mackinac Island share a common history and common goals of public service. With this in mind, it is our great pleasure to support the publication of this story of the park and Park Commission, *100 Years at Mackinac*. We join with Michigan businesses and citizens from around the state in celebrating 100 years of achievement and extending best wishes for the future.

William R. Gregory
President and Chief Executive Officer
Edison Sault Electric Company

100 YEARS AT MACKINAC

THROUGHOUT ITS FIRST 100 YEARS, the Mackinac Island State Park Commission has faced diverse challenges in managing the land, facilities, and programs that constitute our park and museum system. The responsibilities often seem endless—from environmental concerns to preservation of buildings, documents, and artifacts; from operating an airport and enforcing our renowned motor-vehicle ban, to sweeping the streets and helping provide community fire protection; from hosting and serving nearly a million visitors a year to operating world-class museums and advancing educational and historical research.

Earlier commissions struggled with many of these same challenges. The days after the withdrawal of the U.S. Army from Fort Mackinac were marked by shortages of funds and staff. The arrival of the first automobile required judgments and a unique, historic response. The boom of the 1920s and Depression of the 1930s were marked by all kinds of park development schemes, and the war years of the 1940s threatened our buildings with neglect and decay. The 1950s and the years following brought us new challenges, with marked increases in the number of visitors and escalating growth pressures.

Through all of these times, the Mackinac Island State Park Commission has been charged with the stewardship of our unique assets. The Park Commission's goal 100 years ago was preservation of the wonders of Mackinac for the use and enjoyment of generations to come. That remains our goal today. With the help of many we shall achieve the ongoing fulfillment of that objective.

I trust you will enjoy this centennial history, with its fascinating stories of how our parks and museums developed and its sketches of some of the people who contributed to their creation and growth. Our Mackinac parks are now known world-wide for outstanding natural beauty and historical importance. Their future is based on a strong understanding and appreciation of the past. In this centennial year, as our commission remembers its first 100 years, we look forward with you to a new century of preservation and public service.

Dennis O. Cawthorne
Chairman
Mackinac Island State Park Commission

FROM THE DIRECTOR

STARTING IN 1958, the Mackinac Island State Park Commission has created a nationally recognized museum system. The commission cares for and interprets the cultural and natural history of the Straits of Mackinac, and preserves buildings, artifacts, documents and photographs for future generations. Through archaeology and documentary research, the commission uses museum exhibits, programs and publications to tell the stories of the people who have lived at the Straits from prehistoric times to the present. Hundreds of thousands of visitors from around the world visit Mackinac State Historic Parks each year to see and enjoy the treasures and stories of Fort Mackinac, Colonial Michilimackinac and Historic Mill Creek.

Perhaps our greatest historic treasure is one that does not fit inside a museum, and one that is preserved yet continues in daily use. It was for natural beauty and scenic wonders that Mackinac Island State Park was recognized as America's second National Park in 1875 and in 1895 became Michigan's first state park. The park remains the centerpiece of our efforts today.

The story of Mackinac and the Straits is a story of geography. Travel routes along the lakes and rivers first connected Mackinac to European cultures in the 17th century. Great powers fought military battles to control the Straits and Mackinac Island in the 18th and 19th centuries. In our own times, preservation or use of land have been predominant themes. Through its first 100 years, Mackinac Island State Park has retained much of its early character.

The commissioners and staff of the Mackinac Island State Park Commission mark this centennial year by telling the story of these first 100 years in this book, authored by David A. Armour. We join with Mackinac Associates and all who love the Mackinac region in renewing our commitment to park preservation as an essential element of our stewardship of Michigan's most important historic and natural resources.

Carl R. Nold

Carl R. Nold
Director
Mackinac Island State Park Commission

Table of Contents

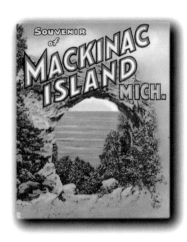

1   How It All Began

THERE IS MAGIC IN MACKINAC, where lakes Michigan and Huron meet in a landscape that was scoured and shaped by mile-thick glaciers. In the 10,000-odd years since the glaciers melted, the water has shaped the limestone core of the land into unusual features which have attracted the attention and wonder of all who have seen them.

Mackinac has been a gathering place almost since the glaciers receded. Dominating the landscape today is Mackinac Island, whose cliffs rise 300 feet from the lake. It resembles a great brooding turtle which bore the world on its back, and the first people who ventured into the area after the ice melted believed it was the place where the world had been born.

Native people came at certain seasons to take whitefish and trout from the waters of the Straits, establishing a seasonal pattern of use that has been the way of Mackinac ever since.

When Europeans arrived thousands of years later, they too recognized its importance as a gathering place. The first Europeans—French missionaries and fur traders—came to the region to stay during the late 17th century. They settled first on the north side of the Straits in what is now Michigan's Upper Peninsula, and early in the 18th century moved to the south side near today's Mackinaw City. After the British took Canada in the French and Indian War, Mackinac came under their control.

When the American colonies revolted, the British moved to the more readily defensible Mackinac Island, and there erected the massive limestone walls of Fort Mackinac. The revolution's success put the Straits in American hands and, except for a brief lapse into British control during the War of 1812, it has been American ever since.

Over time the year-round community at Mackinac Island has grown in fits and starts, but the basic size of the town has remained the same. So has the ancient, seasonal pattern of a small, year-round population that hosts a large influx of summer visitors who come to earn a living or to enjoy the wonders of Mackinac.

During the 19th century the economy of Mackinac shifted from the fur trade to fishing, and then to tourism. By the time of the Civil War, lake boats were bringing visitors to Mackinac to enjoy the "healthy air" or explore the island's natural wonders.

Such was the growing reputation of Macki-

RIGHT: Soldiers evacuating
Fort Mackinac in 1894.

BELOW: The porch of Grand Hotel has
always been a popular gathering spot for
Mackinac Island visitors.

BEFORE 1895

RIGHT: Wildflowers in profusion enliven Mackinac throughout the summer.

BELOW: Fort Mackinac overlooks the town and harbor.

nac Island that Thomas W. Ferry, a Mackinac boy who had grown up to become a U.S. Senator, spearheaded a move to have Congress designate the government land on Mackinac Island as a national park. He succeeded, and in 1875, three years after Yellowstone had become the United States' first national park, Mackinac became the second.

Set aside "for the benefit and enjoyment of the people," the 911 acres outside the 104-acre military reservation were to be maintained by the soldiers who garrisoned Fort Mackinac. The War Department designated the commanding officer as superintendent of the park and gave him an additional company of soldiers to help care for it.

While no funds were provided for park development and operation, the War Department did permit the park to raise money for building roads and bridle paths by granting 10-year leases on "small parcels of ground, at such places in the park as shall require the erection of buildings for the accommodation of visitors." Within a few years, lots were platted on the bluff east of Fort Mackinac and in an area immediately west of Grand Hotel. The first summer cottage on leased land was erected in 1885.

Then, after a group of businessmen built Grand Hotel on private land in 1887, Mackinac became a fashionable resort for the wealthy of Detroit, Chicago and St. Louis, and summer homes began popping up like mushrooms on the leased land near the hotel.

In 1889, using revenue generated by leases, the soldiers built a scenic drive—Leslie Avenue—along the eastern bluff from Arch Rock north to the private Early farm, then west along the Early property line to intersect with British Landing Road, which runs up the center of the island.

The numbers of visitors to the Mackinac area increased after the Michigan Central and the Grand Rapids and Indiana railroads pushed tracks north to Mackinaw City in the early 1880s. Ferries of the Arnold Transit Company met the trains in Mackinaw City and transported expectant visitors to the wonders of the "Fairy Isle of Mackinac."

To accommodate the visitors, entrepreneurs built new hotels and shops and renovated old ones. Guidebooks were published pointing out the historic and natural features, and a host of carriage drivers accosted the visitors, energetically urging them to take horse-drawn scenic tours of the island. By the late 19th century all the elements that made Mackinac the premier tourist location in the midwest were in place, and the future looked bright.

Then disaster struck. In an effort to save money, the U.S. Army decided to consolidate its posts and close Fort Mackinac.

In the 1890s there was no National Park Service. All the national parks were under the War Department and subject to their priorities. While Mackinac was a beautiful and pleasant post enjoyed by the soldiers stationed there, it had no remaining military importance, and its troops were needed in Sault Ste. Marie to guard the canal there. Without the troops, who would care for the National Park?

On October 9, 1894, soldiers from Fort Macki-

ABOVE: The soldiers at Fort Mackinac were the caretakers of Mackinac National Park.

The document transferring Mackinac National Park to the State of Michigan.

nac marched down to waiting boats, leaving only a lieutenant named Woodbridge Geary and a squad of 11 men to guard the fort and park.

Secretary of War Daniel S. Lamont favored selling the government lands, but a group of Mackinac citizens enlisted the aid of Senator James McMillan, who took the lead in developing a plan to keep Mackinac in public ownership. McMillan, a decisive man with a deep interest in park programs, secured the acquiescence of the War Department and lined up support in Congress. In February, 1895, he introduced an amendment to an appropriation bill which would authorize the Secretary of War, "on the application of the governor of Michigan, to turn over to the State of Michigan, for use as a state park, the military reservation and buildings and the lands of the national park." Congress passed the bill on March 2, with the added stipulation that the land would revert to the United States if it ever ceased to be used for park purposes.

Michigan had no state park system, but the state legislature acted quickly, and by joint resolution on May 31, 1895, created the Mackinac Island State Park Commission to manage Michigan's first state park.

Governor John T. Rich immediately appointed the five members of the newly created Commission. Among them was Senator Thomas W. Ferry, by then living in Grand Haven, whose efforts had led to the national park 20 years earlier. The others were William M. Clark of Lansing, Peter White of Marquette, George T. Arnold of Mackinac Island and Albert M. Stephens of Detroit.

The commission first met on July 11 at Grand Hotel on Mackinac Island. Senator Ferry was too ill to attend, but the others nonetheless elected him unanimously as permanent president of the commission. He attended two meetings before he died in 1896. The commissioners chose the energetic White as vice president, Clark as secretary, and Stephens as treasurer. Governor Rich, an ex-officio member of the board, also attended.

The Mackinac Island State Park Commission still had no staff, no money, and no land, and took steps to correct all three shortcomings. Its first official act after electing officers was to authorize a letter to the Secretary of War requesting the appointment of an army officer as temporary park superintendent. Next, the commission doubled the annual lease rents, to $100 for front lots and $60 for rear lots, and halved the terms of the leases from 10 to five years. On July 15, a few days after the first meeting, Governor Rich formally requested the Secretary of War to transfer the park to the state. Secretary Lamont signed the official transfer document and applied his large purple seal on August 3.

The commission also asked Secretary Lamont to turn over to the state all lease revenue collected since March 2—the date Congress authorized turning the Mackinac land over to the state. Lamont rebuffed both that request and the request that an officer be named superintendent, but on September 16, 1895, Lieutenant Woodbridge Geary formally transferred the lands of the military reservation, Fort Mackinac, and the National Park to the State of Michigan.

The state had acquired a treasure.

2 Themes and Precedents

As in 1895, the horse and carriage are the primary method of transport at Mackinac.

THE YEAR 1895, when Mackinac Island became Michigan's first state park, was the threshold of a new era not only for the island but for the nation as a whole. Powerful new technologies and forces were transforming the face of America, and they affected the Mackinac Island State Park from its beginning. Among these were electricity, the telephone, and the automobile. Not far behind would be issues of public health and the environment.

Events in these early years sounded themes that have recurred again and again throughout the park's history. Two of them are financial pressure and its handmaiden, development. Closely related is the theme of constant trade-offs between attracting visitors to the park and protecting the island from them at the same time. From the very first, too, the commission has often found itself trying to balance its own interests with those of the state, the island, and the town.

The new technology reared its head at the commission's first meeting, in the form of a communication from the Mackinac Island Electric Light and Telephone Company. The company asked permission to extend its electric lighting system through the State Park. It would be several years before the commission made a decision—largely because of the complexities of having to act in concert with the municipality of Mackinac Island.

Mackinac Island encompasses approximately 2,100 acres and is eight miles in circumference. In 1895, about half the land was state park. The rest was the Village of Mackinac Island, which became a city in 1900 under a charter that incor-

porated an area extending a mile offshore and including nearby Round Island. Like any other city, it is governed by a locally-elected mayor and council. The exact extent of the authority of the park and city, however, has not always been clear. Even something as fundamental as the boundary between them has occasionally been in dispute. This has not always been a bad thing. At times, both sides found mutual benefit and flexibility in keeping their relationships and boundaries murky and ill-defined. But in all cases some measure of communication and cooperation was essential.

Not all the tenants of leased lots in the park were happy with the commission for doubling the rents at its initial meeting in July, 1895. One of them was Mrs. Phoebe Gehr, whose home on Lot #21, East End, had been the first built in the National Park. She protested that her 10-year lease had been renewed on March 31, 1895, before the state took possession of Mackinac Island lands, and that therefore her rent ought not to be doubled until 1905. She eventually agreed to a compromise, paying the old rate of $50 for a year and then the new, $100 rate in subsequent years. She did not accept the compromise graciously, however, but continued to protest.

These early years of the State Park's existence were not prosperous times. The State Park was born in the midst of the four-year, nationwide depression that followed the Panic of 1893, and money for the new park was not easy to come by.

Nevertheless, by the time commissioners held their second meeting, in Lansing on October 28, 1895, they had received a number of lease

RIGHT: Green areas show the original lands turned over to the State of Michigan in 1895. The rest of the land was private.

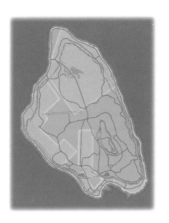

BELOW: View of town from Fort Mackinac in the late 1890s.

renewals at the higher rent. They had managed to accumulate $430, and they hired their first employee—a watchman named John McCarty, Jr., whom they paid the grand sum of $1 a day.

Hoping to generate even more revenue, the commission voted to rent the Captain's Quarters at Fort Mackinac for $350 a year to anyone who would pay two years' rent in advance.

The commission still didn't have enough to

hire a park superintendent, so Commissioner George T. Arnold, a resident of Mackinac Island, took on most of the commission's administrative responsibilities. One of his first tasks was overseeing $100 worth of work on State Park roads. This assumption of administrative duties by one of its members was a precedent to which the commission would return often during lean times.

By the time it met the next May, the com-

RIGHT: Cows graze on the fort pasture.

BELOW: A scenic vista below Robinson's Folly.

mission had enough in its coffers to hire the park's first superintendent. From among several applicants, they chose a Civil War veteran, Capt. Homer L. Thayer of Lansing, and agreed to pay him $800 a year and provide him with a house and a garden. The commission also authorized Thayer to hire three watchmen—for $1.50 a day apiece. The commission even bought a bicycle to help the watchmen get around the park and agreed they should be empowered as deputy sheriffs, since they would be protecting state buildings and lands.

Protection of the park's resources was of mounting concern for both the commissioners and island residents, who knew the commission's primary revenue was from leases on park land and were afraid that historic sites might be ravaged in order to create building locations. Concern was so keen that on August 10, 1896, a number of concerned citizens submitted a petition and letter "relative to retaining the certain historic spots just as they are today and not leasing the same to anyone and [in support of] retaining certain ancient pathways in the vicinity of the fort grounds." Among the petitioners was the Rev. Meade C. Williams, who was writing a historic guidebook to Mackinac Island.

The commission, trying to be sensitive to these concerns, agreed not to lease land in certain areas, including Robinson's Folly, the wooded area immediately east of the fort, and the knoll immediately west of the fort.

However, financial pressure remained intense on the Park Commission. Since it was the island's biggest landowner back then, as it is now, finan-

LEFT: Cottage built by Mrs. S. A. Hert on "Old Fort Garden" lot #3.

cial pressure meant development pressure. At that same meeting in August of 1896, the commissioners received a request to furnish lands near Fort Holmes for a water reservoir and heard a proposal for "a boulevard around the shore of the island" to be named "The State Park Boulevard." A month later, the commission authorized the boulevard, and a subdivision was not far behind. Within two years the commission was surveying lots along the boulevard on the western side of the island. Despite their initial resolve, the commissioners also reneged on part of the promise they made the petitioners, when they agreed to lease the western knoll as a summer-cottage site to Lawrence A. Young

Finances grew especially tight in 1897, especially when some lessees failed to pay rent on time. Just in case, in March that year the Michigan Legislature authorized the commission to give Fort Mackinac and the 103-acre Military Reservation back to the United States "whenever the Secretary of War notified the Commission that it was desired for military occupation." Happily, the authority was never exercised.

To provide additional income, the Park Commission granted concessions in 1897 for souvenir stands at Arch Rock and Fort Holmes. It was not enough, however. That September the commission had to terminate Superintendent Thayer and place Commissioner Arnold in charge again. The next year, the commission even rented out the fort pasture land—on what is now the Grand Hotel golf course. Island residents paid $5 for each cow they pastured there, and in 1898 the commission took in $90 from owners of 18 cows.

The program was not an unalloyed success, for cows frequently caused problems by straying from the pasture into both the village and the park.

By the end of the summer of 1898, the economic picture was brightening, and the Mackinac Island State Park Commission's finances had recovered enough to let the commissioners hire a new superintendent, named Samuel D. Poole. The job was no sinecure; although the commission agreed to pay Poole $50 a month and give him a house on the fort grounds, it did so only with the understanding that he could be terminated at any time on just 30 days' notice. It was hardly job security.

During the late 1890s, the commission was deep into plans for the new subdivision. Known as "Boulevard Western Subdivision," it was to be on land along the island's western shore, some of it state-owned and some on the private Stockbridge estate. The road to it was to be the new lakeshore boulevard which the park and village had authorized in August and September of 1896.

Eventually 24 lots were laid out for lease in the State Park's portion of the subdivision, along with others on the private land. A plat map submitted on August 1, 1898, by St. Ignace surveyor Byron E. Cubley showed a boulevard 40 feet wide along the shore, with building lots on the landward side. The land between the road and lake was left open. Subdivision roads were cleared, as were 12-foot lanes along the lot lines so that prospective lessees could see the lots. A new road, Forest Drive, was even built from the top of the bluff, and 100 copies of the plat were printed and

Postcard of picnickers at Robinson's Folly.

RIGHT: Park staff lived in the former Sergeant's Quarters. They kept cows to provide fresh milk.

FAR RIGHT: East side of the island from Arch Rock.

tacked up around the island, along with promotional posters. All this activity was a bit optimistic, as things turned out. There is no record that any of these lots were ever actually leased.

Forest Drive, however, is still in use, and although the state-owned property is overgrown, signs of the century-old subdivision are still dimly visible in the underbrush. Moreover, now, a century later, the private land that was involved in that ill-fated development has again been developed for sale.

While the "Boulevard Western Subdivision" never came to pass, the shore road to it did. The village approved the acquisition of a right-of-way at least 20 feet wide along the west side of Mackinac Island. Where the route passed through State Park land, the Park Commission cooperated, furnishing the land and assisting in other ways. Over the next few years a major project of both the village and the state would be continuing construction of a shore road completely around Mackinac Island.

During this period, too, some prime land below Fort Mackinac was opened up for development. These lots in the "Old Fort Garden" between the Island House Hotel and Island School (now Indian Dormitory), were platted and approved in 1897 and 1898. Lots were to be leased for at least $100 per year, and the houses erected on them had to be worth at least $3,000. Commissioner George T. Arnold, the island resident who had served as superintendent and who had been on the committee to plat the area, applied to lease one of the lots for his personal home. The homes that were built on these lots are still there.

Not only is Mackinac a beautiful place, it also has a rich and complex history, and 1898 was a turning point of sorts. That year the Park Commission authorized a memorial to Dr. William Beaumont, post surgeon at Mackinac in 1822— the first of the many historical markers and memorials in the State Park today. In the new century soon to dawn, efforts to protect and interpret the region's historical resources would be an important component of the commission's activity.

At the turn of the century the commission reported to Governor Hazen S. Pingree that "Mackinac Island is the most beautiful and healthful resort in the Northwest. It is becoming more the place where the tired teacher, clerk, housekeeper, businessman and farmer go to spend their short vacation of a few days. They can here receive the most rest and benefit in the brief time they have to rest. While the rich can build their palatial cottages on the Island, the people of moderate means are making it more and more their playground and resting spot. The commission desires to make this park and island more emphatically, 'the people's resort.'"

3 Horse Power

T HE MACKINAC ISLAND STATE Park Commission has long had a close working relationship with the island's liverymen, who began providing carriage tours in the mid-19th century, well before there was a park. This is inevitable on an island where automobiles have never been allowed, since the liverymen's horses power the island's transportation system.

Generally, the relationship has been friendly, but it has not always been so, and one of the instances of conflict had effects that go beyond the horse-and-buggy business. It happened in 1901, when commissioners decided that since liverymen benefitted from the commission's road building and maintenance projects, they should help pay for them. At the start of the season that June the commission imposed a yearly license fee of $1 per seat on drivers of vehicles for hire. They also passed a rule barring drivers who did not pay from using park roads for a year.

Though they were accustomed to city regulations, not all the carriage men took kindly to the new State Park rules, and several did not pay. In August the commission directed Park Superintendent Samuel B. Poole to give the delinquents 24 hours to pay or be barred.

One of the drivers, Patrick Kerrigan, paid his $5 for a license, but then filed a suit challenging the fee. The case went all the way to the Michigan Supreme Court, which ruled a year later that the commission "did not exceed its authority in requiring this license fee to be paid." The decision laid a foundation for all subsequent regulation of commercial use of State Park property.

During the 1920s, aggressive tour operators took to overcharging customers and short-cutting tours. Complaints followed and led to the threat of tight regulations, so in hopes of heading off the threat, the tour operators formed a self-regulating association. Its internal discipline worked for many years.

The carriage business on Mackinac was operated for years by local families—23 of them in the 1940s. In 1947, with the promise of a postwar tourist boom, the association incorporated as Mackinac Island Carriage Tours, and the commission granted it an exclusive transportation franchise for the park.

This was especially important in the 1950s, when the commission began charging admission to Fort Mackinac to help pay off bonds for park improvements. The 150-foot bluff leading to the fort was a formidable obstacle, and Mackinac Island Carriage Tours' "buggy with the fringe on top" was the way many visitors got to the fort. The commission depended on the carriages to bring it customers.

William Stewart Woodfill, owner of Grand Hotel and the commission's chairman at the time, was the mastermind behind the ambitious development of tourism on Mackinac in the 1950s. Among other things, he sought significant improvements in the horse-drawn transportation system. He insisted that all drivers be in uniform, and that they give their customers accurate information about the island and the park. Drivers who refused to cooperate were brought into Woodfill's office for a formal hearing, and were either warned or given a 24-hour suspen-

William Shine's license badge.

ABOVE LEFT:
Riders at Fort
Holmes.

LEFT: An island
cottager out for a
ride with her
horse and dogs at
the turn of the
century.

HORSE POWER

RIGHT: Commercial carriages must have a license to operate within the State Park.

BELOW: Mackinac Island Carriage Tours transports over 200,000 visitors each year.

sion. A park policeman was hired to oversee the enforcement of the carriage rules.

After public hearings, limits were set on the number of carriages of various kinds that would be allowed. Only 55 sightseeing carriages were permitted, along with eight taxicabs, 18 drive-yourself carriages, seven livery carriages, and two Fort Mackinac buses. Some numbers have hardly changed. The number of sightseeing tour carriages allowed remains at 55, and the number of drive-yourself carriages at 18. The number of liveries allowed has been increased to 21 (although fewer than that actually operate) and the limit on taxis is now 17.

To increase the number of tours a given carriage could make in a day, the commission built new, short-cut roads that shaved precious minutes off the time it took to complete a tour. One such road ran from Skull Cave across the Rifle Range to Sugar Loaf Road. Now named "Rifle Range Road," it was later extended to Crooked Tree Road, eliminating Sugar Loaf from the tours. Another new road, from Fort Holmes to Skull Cave, was so steep it was dubbed "Suicide Hill." Eventually the whole loop to Point Lookout and Fort Holmes was eliminated from the standard tour, and "Suicide Hill" was closed to vehicular traffic. Today, it's a footpath named "Henry Trail."

By commission regulation, the carriage tours had to stop at least nine minutes at Arch Rock. This was partly so visitors could see the arch and nearby Nicolet's Watchtower and use the rest rooms nearby, but largely so they would have time to buy something at the souvenir stand there. The commission razed the souvenir stand in 1972 in an effort to make the setting more natural, and the rule no longer applies. Commission regulations still required a stop, however, at the Fort Mackinac Avenue of Flags, where an attendant welcomes guests to tour the fort. About a third of the passengers take advantage of this opportunity to visit the fort without walking up the hill.

During the 1980s, the tour routine changed after Carriage Tours developed a new, 35-passenger carriage, pulled by three massive horses, to operate only on the relatively flat plateau at the Fort Mackinac level. Smaller, 18-passenger carriages bring visitors up from the town on the first leg of the tour to a depot named Surrey Hill, where they transfer to the larger rigs. After a circuit of the cemeteries, Rifle Range, Arch Rock, Fort Mackinac and the Governor's Summer Residence, they return to Surrey Hill to board the smaller carriages for the ride back downtown.

Each year approximately 200,000 island visitors ride on the official Mackinac Island Carriage Tours, but there are other options for people wanting a horse-and-buggy ride. Old-fashioned liveries line up on the street in front of Marquette Park and charge by the hour to take passengers anywhere on the island. In addition, horse taxis operate 24 hours a day, charging fixed point-to-point fares. The more adventurous can

Bicycles have long been a common form of transportation on Mackinac Island, which blossomed as a resort about the same time in the 1880s that the newly invented "modern" bicycle was enjoying a boom all across the nation. After the island's Lake Shore Drive was paved in 1960, bicycles became so popular among visitors that, in 1964, the State Park Commission grew concerned about safety. For a time, the commission limited the number of rental bicycles to 825. But, when the limit was challenged by a new business that wanted to have additional licenses, the commission responded by turning the licensing of bicycles over to the city. Today, a number of vendors on the island rent bicycles, including bicycles built for two, and the eight-mile ride around the island on Lake Shore Drive is still a favorite.

HORSE POWER

ABOVE: Carriages for hire on Main Street in 1908.

hire small, one-horse, "drive-yourself" carriages. The island also has 70 saddle horses available for rent by the hour.

Mackinac Island Carriage Tours Inc. still operates all the sightseeing tours, under its long-term franchise. It also operates most of the taxis and about half the liveries. The rest of the island's "carriage trade" consists of various, independent licensees. The island's freight is hauled primarily by two types of horse-drawn dray. The general freight wagons are flat-bed drays with low sides that fold down. High-sided trash wagons haul the island's refuse.

On an island where the horse is king, flies can lead a princely life. They were a constant problem on Mackinac until DDT was developed in World War II to protect GIs from jungle insects. After the war, the state and the City of Mack-

inac Island undertook a joint spraying program. It meant using a truck, and was done in the wee hours to keep visitors from knowing a motor vehicle was being used. DDT fell from favor on environmental grounds as islanders noticed that Mackinac's bird population had declined and as flies developed resistance to it. The Park Commission sent a colony of island flies to East Lansing so Michigan State University scientists could test them for resistance to other chemicals that were tried, including chlordane, Cygon and malathion. Eventually, MSU scientists developed a chemical-free plan to combine strict, island-wide sanitation with the release of tiny, parasitic wasps which feed on fly eggs. Today, with the rules enforced by a city-employed "fly control officer," the plan still works well, and flies are no longer a serious problem on Mackinac.

Horse-drawn transportation generates a considerable amount of waste of its own, and the island's commercial haulers contribute to a street-cleaning program that picks up manure and flushes the pavements.

Humane treatment of the island's horses has been a matter of interest to the commission for many years, and in the park's early years, the animals were not always well cared for. In 1930 the State Department of Agriculture sent a veterinarian to look out for them, and the commission provided housing for the vet. But with the formation of Mackinac Island Carriage Tours, Inc. the care of horses greatly improved. In the mid-1960s, the state stopped provided housing for the vets.

4 # The New Century

In 1900 this new road scraper proved very useful in the construction of park roads.

IN THE EARLY YEARS of the Mackinac Island State Park Commission, most of the funds raised from leases and rents were devoted to building and improving roads. One was the boulevard built along the west shore in the 1890s to connect the town to the island's north end. Until then, the only route had been British Landing Road, whose name derived from the War of 1812, when British invaders landed at the north end and dragged cannons to the heights above Fort Mackinac and forced an American surrender.

Once the new shore road along the west side of the island had been built, the idea of another shore road caught the commission's imagination. This one would run below the cliffs of the island's east side.

Building such a road would not be easy, because the waters of Lake Huron lapped directly against rocks at the base of the cliffs there. But Superintendent Poole and Commissioner William A. Perrin paddled along the east shore to reconnoiter the route, and they reported that the road could—and should—be built.

On August 10, 1900, the commission agreed to build the road as far as John Early's farm. Later, they received a 30-foot-wide easement from Early to continue the road over his land. Once finished, the road would join the west shore road and encircle the island.

Road construction on such a scale cost a lot more than the commission's meager revenues allowed. That year it was considered a major expenditure when the commission paid $395 to the Indiana Road Machine Company for a new scraper. Much more than that would be needed for this project. The commission got it when the legislature approved a $10,000 loan, which would be repaid from future revenue. For the next few years the park superintendent supervised a sizeable crew that built the shore road along the island's east side.

It would all be worth it, the commission felt. The road, the commission told Governor Aaron T. Bliss in its 1901 report, "will be unsurpassed for beauty and perfection of road-way by any drive on the earth, and will add greatly to the attractions on the Island for those enjoying driving or wheeling."

The commission was right. The new roads, used primarily by carriage men who drove tourists on scenic tours of the island, made the driving easier and opened up new areas of great beauty.

ROAD TO BRITISH LANDING, MACKINAC ISLAND, MICH.

EVENTUALLY, OF COURSE, all these efforts to attract visitors paid off handsomely. In a way, the payoff was too handsome, because the commission also found itself in need of new laws to help preserve those "areas of great beauty." Fortunately, by 1901, the Michigan Legislature had taken notice of that, too, and not only made it a misdemeanor to litter or to damage trees on the island, but gave the com-

mission power to appoint special police to enforce the laws.

Unfortunately, there was nothing in the law about the aesthetics of such things as telephone poles. The telephone was the first "modern" utility system installed on Mackinac, and the Mackinac Island Electric Light and Telephone Co. was so careless about what its poles looked like that the commission had to request that the poles be

The deserted Soldiers' Barracks at Fort Mackinac.

moved, or placed along the rear lot lines.

The early growth of utilities demonstrated the intertwining of private, municipal, and state interests on a place like Mackinac. A succession of water companies applied for and received franchises from the city and State Park, but the project floundered through the late 1890s for lack of financial backing, and cottagers on the East Bluff asked the park to furnish water to them. The state-owned park water system, installed some years before by the Army, drew its water from a spring below the fort's West Blockhouse. From a pump house there, water was piped up to a tank in the upper story of the North Blockhouse, from which it flowed by gravity to the buildings of the fort. In 1900, the State Park extended a small line to serve cottages on the East Bluff and new cottages planned on the newly platted Fort Garden lots. To recoup their costs the state charged cottagers $10 "water rent."

In 1901 the waterworks company finally secured financing and built its own pump house and a reservoir. The pump house and intake were on the same site as the electrical generation plant, and the reservoir was on high ground near Fort Holmes that was in the State Park. Moreover, the 60-man crew that built the private water system lived in rented buildings in the park-owned fort, and the Park Commission furnished free gravel and sand for the project.

FOR ALL THE WORK ON ROADS and utilities, the Park Commission spent only a limited amount of money during its first few years on building maintenance. Nonethe-

less, in acquiring the park from the War Department in 1895, the commission accepted not only 40 buildings, but also the responsibility of maintaining them. A few had been renovated so they could be rented out. The roof on the former Commanding Officer's house, for instance, was raised to make the loft into a full second story so the building could be rented to a Mrs. Fannie O. Lathrop. The fort buildings were also painted white to cover the military's browns.

By 1903, however, many of the buildings were badly in need of repair. Not yet in a position to afford to keep all that property up, the young commission sought—and found—a new source of revenue: the state itself. The commission spelled out its case in some detail in its annual report dated May 1, 1903: "The act creating the Commission makes it the duty of the Commission to preserve and keep in repair the Fort and the buildings. To do this with our present revenues, and keep up the drives, roads, and park is impossible . . . The fort wall shows signs of weakening in a number of places—either the mortar was poor, or its strength has gone. The decayed woodwork of the fort about the walls—parapet, blockhouses, and gates—must be replaced. Buildings must be repaired, roofed and painted."

Then, adding that "these repairs must be made or the State disgraced and the terms of the grant from the United States violated," the commissioners asked for an appropriation of $5,000.

They got it, and on June 20, 1904, received the first $1,500 for a new General Repair Fund. Another $2,000 followed the next January, and once the whole $5,000 was spent, a new appro-

priation for $12,000 was forthcoming in 1907 to the commission's General Improvement Fund.

Buildings were not the only thing on the island in need of upkeep. Early in the new century the commission received complaints about the condition of the former Army Post Cemetery, as well. These were passed on to the War Department, but the Army's Major and Quarter Master, Major J. T. French, politely told the commission that the cemetery had become the state's along with the rest of the old military property. "All expenses in connection with the maintenance of the Post Cemetery at Old Fort Mackinac," he wrote, "are to be borne by the State of Michigan." The commission bit the bullet and spent $200 of its own funds to improve the cemetery, too.

The War Department was not nearly so tight-fisted when it came to dressing up the old fort, however. When the commissioners began fixing up the buildings there, they recognized that the absence of cannons detracted from the appearance of the place and asked the War Department to provide some. Apparently the Army needed its old cannons less than its money, and in 1905 it sent along several from Sault Ste. Marie so the state could re-arm Fort Mackinac.

Restoring history has long held high priority in the operations of the Mackinac Island State Park Commission. During the early refurbishment of buildings, one of the structures being fixed up was a barn in the fort garden. The barn, the story went, had been built with timbers left over when the old blockhouse at Fort Holmes was taken down in the 1820s. The commission decided to take the timbers back up to Fort Holmes and rebuild the blockhouse, which might attract people to Mr. E. W. Wallace's curio stand. Mr. Wallace approved of the idea, and in 1905 he paid for a new roof and windows.

This sort of concern for the history of Fort Mackinac was fostered by Dr. John R. Bailey, who was appointed to the commission in 1903. Dr. Bailey, then 80 years old, had served as post surgeon at Fort Mackinac more than 20 times since 1854. After retiring from the Army, he lived on Mackinac Island, where he had a private practice, ran Bailey's National Park Drugstore, and served twice as village president. In 1895, he published *Mackinac Formerly Michilimackinac: History and Guidebook*, which saw many later editions. Dr. Bailey's long, flowing, white beard made him a distinctive personality on the island, and during his seven years on the commission he remained active and energetic and keenly interested in preserving island history.

PRIVATE DEVELOPMENT GREW quickly on Mackinac early in the 20th century, and when it involved land adjacent to the park, the commission had to maintain constant vigilance for trespasses onto state land.

When the east wing of Grand Hotel was expanded at one point, the manager of the hotel, a Mr. Henry Weaver, had a stone property marker moved, and then erected a fence on park land. Superintendent Poole confronted him, but Weaver just laughed it off. The park hired a surveyor in 1905 to document the trespass, and a more extensive survey in 1913 confirmed the

ABOVE, FAR LEFT: Large rocks which fell from Robinson's Folly provide convenient resting places.

ABOVE, LEFT: In 1905 the War Department donated several obsolete cannons to re-arm Fort Mackinac.

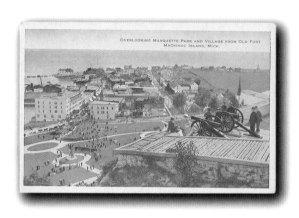

Dr. John R. Bailey in his flowing white beard awaits the unveiling of the statue of Father Marquette.

park boundaries. When the Chippewa Hotel was erected on the waterfront adjacent to State Park land in 1902, one corner of the hotel extended across the lot line onto State Park land because of careless surveying. The trespass was documented by a subsequent survey and required the park to issue an annual use permit that acknowledged the trespass across State Park boundaries.

Over the years, as superintendents have come and gone, the State Park administration has alternated between watchfulness and forgetfulness where the boundaries are concerned. Trespasses during lax periods have led to later reliance on use permits and, in some cases, have meant lengthy litigation.

One of the most egregious cases came many years later and led to the loss of a lovely 36-acre tract with half a mile of waterfront, called Brown's Brook. In 1965, during airport construction on state land, storm runoff eroded land below the bluff that was jointly owned by the park and an organization called Moral Re-Armament. When the organization sued for damages, the Park Commission neglected to point out that it was part owner of the property. That opened the door in the 1970s for the Burton Abstract Company to claim full ownership by right of "adverse possession"—the concept that if a trespasser goes unchallenged long enough, the land becomes his. The case, which reached the State Supreme Court, resulted in the state's losing its right to the beautiful tract. State efforts to repurchase the land failed, and today the land is being privately developed as residences. It should never happen again; Michigan now has laws to prevent

anyone's claiming state land by right of adverse possession.

The Park Commission was not always so neglectful. In concerning itself early in the century with park boundaries, the commission began to question the status of several tracts to which title was unclear. One parcel that attracted their attention was the "Borough Lot," eight acres that the U.S. Government had given the Borough of Michilimackinac (now the City of Mackinac Island) in 1818 "for public purposes." In the 1880s, when investors were planning Grand Hotel, the city gave them a 99-year lease on the lot as an inducement to build. The Park Commission, however, felt that by leasing the land for private purposes the city had violated the terms of the original grant and that the lot should revert to the United States. And since all U.S. property on Mackinac Island had been granted to the state in 1895, the Park Commission argued, the Borough Lot should revert to the state as the custodian of former federal lands. While the argument failed and the Borough Lot remained the city's, the park commissioners' claim did not win them many friends among village officials or Grand Hotel investors.

At one point in 1905, in examining old land records, the commission noted that many of the original deeds reserved a 100-foot strip along the beach for public use. However, a number of buildings had been built on this land, particularly in the harbor area. This remained an issue for 30 years after the extensive 1913 survey confirmed the trespasses, as the commission sought to gain title to the waterfront strip through action of the

OPPOSITE, LEFT AND BELOW: The unveiling of the bronze Marquette statue on August 4, 1909, was one of the most photographed events in Mackinac's history. Cameras recorded the event for posterity from all angles as the crowd of well dressed onlookers cheered.

The Fort Mackinac Post Cemetery.

Attorney General and U.S. Congress.

One of the partners in the Chippewa Hotel when it was built on waterfront land adjacent to the park in 1902, was one of the original park commissioners, George T. Arnold. Such mixed public-private involvement on the island is hardly unusual. In midsummer of 1903 Superintendent Samuel B. Poole resigned but stayed on Mackinac and built another hotel. This one, on the water at the west end of the harbor, was later substantially expanded and became the Iroquois Hotel.

POOLE'S REPLACEMENT as superintendent was B. Frank Emery of Detroit. Paid $800 a year plus the remodeled Hill Quarters in Fort Mackinac as a residence, he remained six years. Near the end of his term, change came wholesale to the Park Commission.

In 1908, three of the five commissioners died, including Peter White, another of the original five, who had been a driving force in the park's early days and the commission's president more than 11 years. It was largely his interest and energy that led to establishment of Marquette Park, and his fund-raising provided for the statue there of Father Marquette. Indeed, at his death, the commission went on record as saying that it was largely due to White's "farsightedness and love for Mackinac Island" that the island "was preserved to the people of the state not only for the

present but for future generations."

Commissioners Henry L. Kanter and Charles R. Miller also died in 1908. The three new commissioners named by Governor Fred M. Warner to replace them were Peter White's son-in-law, Alfred O. Jopling of Marquette, Leo M. Butzel of Detroit, and Ira A. Adams of Bellaire.

During 1907 and 1908, substantial additional appropriations by the Michigan Legislature let the Park Commission undertake numerous projects. Besides the road work, the commission made major improvements to the new Marquette Park, laying an eight-foot-wide cement walk and retaining wall in front of it and erecting 14 electric light posts decorated with bronze castings of the Park Commission seal.

Eventually, even Uncle Sam came through to help keep up the old Army Post Cemetery. After repeated requests, Congress appropriated $1,000 to make a one-time grant to the Army's quartermaster general for cemetery improvements. New headstones replaced deteriorated markers and a cannon from Fort Sumter was mounted in the center of the grounds. In time for a dedication on Memorial Day, May 28, 1907, a bronze tablet was put in place. It bears these words of the poet Theodore O'Hara:

On fame's eternal camping ground,
Their silent tents are spread,
And glory guards with solemn round,
The bivouac of the dead.

RIGHT AND BELOW: Anne's Tablet remains a restful place to remember Mackinac Island's most famous fictional heroine.

The bronze plaque commemorating Territorial Governor Lewis Cass.

missioner Wood himself bought the $150 bronze plaque. The memorial was erected at the "Nicolet Watch Tower," a limestone outcropping near Arch Rock, at a ceremony attended by dignitaries and marked by long speeches and an audience-participation singing of "My Country, 'Tis of Thee."

The second marker attributed to Judge Wood was unveiled six weeks later, this honoring Lewis Cass (1782-1866), governor of the Michigan Territory from 1813 to 1831 and secretary of war in President Andrew Jackson's cabinet from 1831 to 1836. The plaque was to be placed east of Fort Mackinac, in a spot named "Cass Cliff." President Woodrow Wilson was invited to the "Lewis Cass Day" ceremony, but could not attend. Hundreds did attend, and Superintendent Kenyon called the event "purely a democratic doin's." He noted that he would rather have attended the Charlevoix Country Club banquet that day, but decided: "This is a case of 'duty before Love,' and [I] will do my duty." Governor Woodbridge N. Ferris addressed the crowd at Fort Mackinac, then adjourned with other VIPs to a reception at Grand Hotel.

The Michigan Historical Commission, delighted with the public exposure generated by these Mackinac Island events, published three bulletins in 1916 commemorating the historical place names on Mackinac Island and reporting the speeches and events.

Not all memorials on the island were the commission's doing. In 1916 Samuel Mather and his sister, of Cleveland, erected a tablet in memory of author Constance Fenimore Woolson, who

had written a number of books and short stories featuring Mackinac Island. Her most famous was the novel, *Anne*, whose fictional heroine lived on Mackinac Island. The Clevelanders deposited $1,000 with Superior Savings and Trust Company, pledging the interest to maintain the tablet site. Mather gave very detailed instructions about how he wished the area to be maintained. The memorial, known as Anne's Tablet, is on the bluff in the woods between Fort Mackinac and the East Bluff. Refurbished in 1994, it remains a popular spot.

Numerous other markers adorn Mackinac Island Park lands. In 1931, the Daughters of the American Revolution of Michigan erected a stone cairn in Marquette Park, to display a bronze tablet proclaiming Mackinac "Michigan's most historic spot."

One of the markers is a high-relief bronze tablet, erected in 1936, depicting Major Andrew Hunter Holmes. He was killed in the 1814 Battle of Mackinac Island, and is remembered now in the name of Fort Holmes, on high ground overlooking Fort Mackinac.

After Governor Frank D. Fitzgerald died in office in 1939, the Park Commission memorialized him with a bronze plaque in the garden in front of the fort cottage that governors used in those days when they stayed on the island.

In the late 1950s the Michigan Historical Commission embarked on an aggressive program for marking historical sites around the State, and approached the Park Commission regarding a number of locations on State Park lands. The markers erected under the program are familiar sights along Michigan roadsides. The Park Commission was not at all certain, at first, that it wanted them. Ever sensitive to maintaining its statutory authority, the commission was wary of anything that might diminish its stature. Commissioners went on record as insisting that the markers not "omit mentioning that the property was part of, and under the jurisdiction of, The Mackinac Island State Park Commission." The concerns were overcome by attaching the Park Commission's official seal to the markers. Since then, more than 15 of the cast aluminum markers have been erected in the commission's parks.

6   The Kenyon Years

ON JUNE 4, 1909, when it accepted responsibility for 20 acres in Mackinaw City, the Mackinac Island State Park Commission found itself in charge for the first time of land that was not on Mackinac Island.

This acreage, known then as "Wawatam Park," was the site of the 18th-century Fort Michili-

mackinac. It had been a public park since Mackinaw City was platted in the 1850s, and in 1904, Mackinaw City had given the land to the State of Michigan. After it languished in limbo five years, the legislature decided to rename it "Michilimackinac State Park" and give it to the Mackinac Island State Park Commission to manage.

Postcard of Michilimackinac State Park

This did not exactly delight the commission. The country was grappling again with econom-ic hard times, and the state had already cut the park's general appropriation in half. Now, the state told the commissioners they had to spend five percent of what was left on the new Mack-inaw City park. After extending all park regula-tions to Michilimackinac, the Park Commission named two special policemen—Vine Harding and Frank Potter—to enforce them, but without pay. The commission did spend $352.53 getting the park ready for a formal acceptance ceremo-ny that Governor Fred M. Warner would attend. But from then until 1913 little more was spent on Michilimackinac, and most funds placed in the Michilimackinac account were returned to the commission's general improvement fund.

Whether it was because of all this is not on record, but at the end of that summer Park Super-intendent B. F. Emery resigned. The man the Park Commission appointed as his replacement, Frank A. Kenyon of East Jordan, Michigan, would play a prominent role in commission affairs for more than 20 years.

Kenyon was a man of strong personality, great energy, and practical skills, who also had the politician's ability to keep in close, personal touch with commissioners and governors. He knew how to trumpet his own achievements, too, and his periodic superintendent's reports are a delight to the historian for their detail.

Kenyon was probably not much bothered by the new Michilimackinac responsibilities. A man of vision, he always kept his ears open for word of land that might be available for addition to the park. During his superintendency Mackinac Island State Park experienced some of its great-est expansion.

Kenyon was a take-charge superintendent, too, and after appointing him, the commission did not meet again for a year and a half. When they finally did meet, in April, 1911, it was because the financial situation had gone from mere crunch to full-blown crisis. The commis-sion's main order of business that day was to name a committee "to confer with Supt. Kenyon about what arrangements can be made for the care of the Island during the summer in view of the veto-ing of the appropriation bill."

The new park superintendent, it appeared, would earn his $1,500-a-year salary the hard way. After seven years of appropriations by the legis-lature, the Park Commission was again faced with operating solely on receipts from rents, leases and

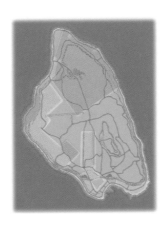

BELOW: Devil's Kitchen, which was donated to the State Park in 1918, with two of superintendent Kenyon's benches.

RIGHT: Fort Mackinac was a frequent venue for public gatherings.

Frank A. Kenyon, superintendent from 1909-1931.

licenses. It was not much to work with. Total receipts for the fiscal year 1911-1912 were only $6,373. After meeting other essential expenses, the park could not even make the year's payment on the road-building loan it had received from the state a decade earlier, on which the commission still owed $2,000 plus interest. Worse, no funds were available for the new park in Mackinaw City.

Superintendent Kenyon waded right in. He tried increasing revenues by selling gravel from state land, and raising potatoes and turnips on the former military parade ground north of the fort. On November 17, 1912, he noted receipts of $144.50 from these efforts.

Kenyon realized, too, that he could save money by cutting planks and boards from trees which had been blown down in storms or felled for road building. Around 1915 he spent $184 to buy a small sawmill with a 12-horsepower engine, and over the years it furnished a considerable amount of lumber for the park. The mill's operations meshed well with the park work program, because it could be run during the winter when many other tasks were impossible.

In the effort to raise money, the commission reluctantly granted a concession for $100 a year for a seasonal ice cream parlor on the Fort Mackinac grounds, at the same time declaring "that hereafter the policy of the commission is against renting fort property for any such purpose." The commission also received modest but welcome help from the City of Mackinac Island, which appropriated $300 towards the maintenance of Marquette Park.

Although complaints flowed in to Governor Chase S. Osborn's office after he vetoed the Mackinac Island State Park appropriations, they fell on unsympathetic ears. "If proper business methods were used," the governor replied, "it seems to me there is no reason why the park should not be self-supporting."

The commission's and Kenyon's dogged efforts to reduce programs did not go unnoticed by the island's summer cottagers, and on September 8, 1911, the Cottagers' Association met at the John Jacob Astor House Hotel to air complaints about the way the beleaguered commission and superintendent were running the park. They particularly resented Kenyon's raising crops on the "famous old parade ground." The cottagers drafted their own petition to the governor, the Park Commission, and the city council which concluded, "While we have no personal feelings against anyone we feel and feel strongly that the Board of Commissioners through their agent, the superintendent, have this year shown their utter disregard and lack of reverence for the history, traditions and sentiment which clings to and makes us love this Beautiful Island."

While Superintendent Kenyon was worried enough to discuss the complaints in person with Governor Osborn, he also met the cottagers head-on at a meeting in his office. Not very subtly, he told them "that in all probability their rental charges would in time be fixed at such an amount as to meet all necessary expenses of maintenance of the state park, as they were the ones who derived the most benefit."

There was "some opposition at first," Kenyon

LEFT: The Fort Mackinac Hill Quarters was converted into a single family residence and used by the park superintendent until 1968.

reported, "but even now some of them are frank to say their rentals are comparatively cheap."

In 1914, the U.S. Coast Guard became interested in constructing a life saving station on the beach immediately east of the Chippewa Hotel, and the Park Commission granted permission for the facility in 1914. A reverter clause in the land transfer proved very important in 1969, when the Coast Guard no longer wanted the building and the land reverted to the state. The old Coast Guard station now houses the State Park Visitor's Center and public restrooms.

By his strict economies, Superintendent Kenyon was able to operate the park within its income while continuing to maintain the roads, trails and buildings. He reduced the park's use of electricity and eventually discontinued it entirely. He never lost sight of his expansion plans, but held them in abeyance for the time being, until funds might again be forthcoming from the state.

Kenyon's future-oriented outlook meshed well with that of Alfred O. Jopling, the Park Commission's newly elected chairman. Jopling, a commissioner since 1908, fell ill and tried to resign in 1911 after being elected chairman, but his fellow commissioners insisted he continue. It was good that he did, for Jopling, like Kenyon, was a man of vision. Both men realized that the commission needed not just more money, but also a master plan.

The park soon got both. The new governor elected in 1912, Woodbridge N. Ferris, was more friendly to the park than his predecessor and did not veto the Park Commission's appropriation. Michigan's only Democratic governor in the 40 years between 1893 and 1933, Ferris served only three years, but he started money flowing again to Mackinac. In each of the next two years the park received $8,379. The commission not only paid off that 1901 road-improvement loan and started fixing up the new Michilimackinac State Park, it had enough left over to hire some expert planners.

One of the planners was Morgan H. Wright, a Marquette, Michigan, surveyor to whom the commission paid $3,575 to survey both the island and Michilimackinac State Park. He drew very detailed maps, erected monuments to mark all park boundaries, and identified all trespasses by developers onto State Park land. Wright's carefully drawn map has proven to be very accurate and has been the basis for all subsequent surveys done on Mackinac Island. State Geologist Dr. R. C. Allen used the map to make a topographical and geological map of the island. Perhaps the most spectacular long-term effect of that survey and mapping was that in revealing evidence of the exact site of Fort Michilimackinac, it alerted the commission to the archaeological potential of its new park in Mackinaw City.

The Park Commission's historical consciousness was raised by the appointment of Judge Edwin O. Wood of Flint to the commission in 1913. He had also been appointed to the then-new Michigan Historical Commission, and helped forge close bonds between these two agencies. Over the next few years the two commissions would co-sponsor commemorative events and work together to establish a State Museum in the Fort Mackinac Officers' Quarters. Using

RIGHT: The State Park crew with the hose cart inside Fort Mackinac.

By the early 1920s Fort Mackinac was becoming dilapidated, and the porch had been removed from the Soldiers' Barracks at right.

Morgan Wright's detailed map as a reference, the Historical Commission suggested historical names for points of interest on the island, such as Haldimand Bay, Biddle Point, Mission Point, and Cass Cliff.

A Boston landscape designer of national reputation, Warren H. Manning, drew plans for future development of both Mackinac Island and Michilimackinac State Parks. He also developed plans for the restoration of some of the park's historic buildings, including the Officers' Stone Quarters. One of the immediate results of his plan was the removal of a number of old military buildings outside the fort to reduce maintenance expenses. The bakery, coal shed, blacksmith shop, scale house, and brick magazine were removed by April, 1914.

With the resumption of appropriations, Superintendent Kenyon spent $2,657 to erect a new horse barn, 48 by 96 feet and with walls 13-1/2 feet high. It was made of poured concrete mixed by hand in large wooden troughs. Kenyon liked to use poured concrete. He also built a concrete vault attached to the former post schoolhouse, which served as the Superintendent's office, as well as a small shed in the revised deer park, a combination tool and chicken house, a concrete watering basin large enough for several deer to stand in, and 25 concrete benches. Kenyon's hard work—which remains in evidence still—was rewarded by a raise in his annual salary from $1,500 to $1,600.

The hired, expert planners also addressed the question of forest fires, which were a continuing concern to the commission. Fear of fire was not unfounded; disastrous blazes swept parts of Michigan and Wisconsin in the early years of the century, and the possibility of a major fire on Mackinac was always in the back of people's minds. Although the island's new water system included some fire hydrants, the island had little firefighting equipment except for one horse-drawn, steam-powered pumper. The Park Commission purchased hose carts and stationed them around the island, including one inside Fort Mackinac. A few standpipes were erected along the island's roads mainly to provide water for sprinkling the surface, but they could also be used, if need be, for fighting fires.

F. H. Sanford of the Department of Forestry at Michigan Agricultural College recommended cutting fire lanes to protect the Island, and Manning's park plan indicated clearings and fire breaks. Park crews also cleared deadwood and brush for 100 feet on either side of roads.

Two breaks cleared in 1913 were the old rifle range from Fort Mackinac to Fort Holmes and the 1,000-yard rifle range near Sugar Loaf. (All the clearing and cutting attracted the attention of the island's cottagers, and 24 of them, led by E. W. Puttkammer, signed a petition of protest, but work went on unabated.)

One of the most interesting questions raised by Morgan Wright's 1913 survey was whether Arch Rock could last. From the time the island's early European visitors discovered this formation, there has been speculation about when it might collapse. Many predicted its imminent demise—including, apparently, surveyor Wright, who wrote that "the destruction of the arch by

weathering seemed not very remote." It has not happened yet, of course, and over the years the commission has sponsored frequent examinations of the arch, usually by the state geologist. On a few occasions concrete has been used to make repairs at the base of the arch and to fill cracks at the top. (In 1972, to make the setting of the area around Arch Rock more "natural," the commission canceled the souvenir concession there and razed the concession stand.)

IN HIS MACKINAC ISLAND PARK master plan the landscape architect, Manning, identified lands that he recommended be added to the State Park's 1,041 acres, and in the next 15 years or so, much of it was acquired. Some parcels, however, came more easily than others.

One of the easiest to acquire was in 1918. While the Park Commission was still developing support among legislators for funds with which to buy lands, the park acquired a major new tract as a gift, from the heirs of a man named Gurdon Hubbard. Hubbard had come to Mackinac a century before as an employee of the American Fur Company, and later made and lost fortunes in business in Chicago. In 1882 he platted a cottage subdivision on the island called "Hubbard's Annex," and in November, 1918, Mrs. E. M. Williams and others of his heirs offered to give the park some of that land. The tract included the limestone sea cave known as Devil's Kitchen, and the Park Commission happily accepted it.

At the same November meeting the Commission discussed another 23 acres for sale on the island. This acquisition turned out to be much more difficult.

Through Superintendent Kenyon and newly appointed Commissioner John P. Hemmeter, a Detroit cigar manufacturer, the commission had been negotiating to buy these 23 acres for more than a year. It had proved quite complicated, however. The parcel was the eastern part of a 40-acre tract that had been owned by a family named Mulcrone. The western 17 acres had been purchased by James Doud, owner of the island's Doud Mercantile Company. The eastern parcel adjoined State Park lands and a corner of it crossed British Landing Road north of the cemeteries, so whoever owned it might block the road. Knowing the park had no money for buying land, but realizing the importance of the parcel, Commissioner Hemmeter bought the land himself for $2,000, to hold until the state might buy it.

Doud, meanwhile, had begun lumbering on his western parcel, leading the Park Commission to fear he might eventually clear the entire 17 acres. Hemmeter tried to persuade Doud to stop cutting trees, but without much success. Continued cutting, he warned Doud in a letter, "would lessen the beauty of the Island, which draws so many tourists and summer residents whose expenditures are really the life blood of the native business public."

Doud, although himself a member of that "native business public," was unimpressed. He wrote back that he planned to make a pasture for milk cows and to plant some fruit trees "in place of the jungle that is now upon the land."

Hemmeter, appalled by Doud's response, wrote

BELOW: Wawashkamo golf
course club house on the Peter
Early farm.

back that "virgin timber, the pride of the Island, can be cut in a very short time, but it would require more than half a century to replace it if it should prove a mistake. It seems a pity to cut such timber when the tax payers of the State are paying thousands of dollars for reforestation." The Park Commission, Hemmeter added, "is very anxious to enlarge the State Property and improve and beautify it . . . I am pleading with you not to

destroy what we are trying to build up, and preserve, and that which nature has so kindly and generously given to Mackinac Island."

Still without funds for buying land, the commission sent a committee to Lansing to seek an appropriation, and the parcel Hemmeter acquired was finally purchased in 1920 by the state. Even after the commission had the new tract surveyed, Doud disputed the boundary. The next year, when

A36—A SUMMER AFTERNOON IN MARQUETTE PARK, MACKINAC ISLAND, MICH.

Superintendent Kenyon began to erect a fence, Doud waved a gun at him and accused him of trespass. Then Doud filed suit to stop the fence until the boundary line was settled. The case lingered in court for nearly 10 years before the exact boundary was finally determined by court action in 1930.

During the 1920s the Park Commission's agents spent a lot of time in court regarding land matters, and some of the cases ended with the park's losing land rather than acquiring it. The most celebrated was the case of that 100-foot strip along the waterfront that the Morgan Wright survey of 1913 had pointed out.

The survey showed that the deeds to much of the private land on Mackinac Island reserved a 100-foot strip along the shore for public use. Over the years, however, many structures had been built on this strip, particularly in the harbor area. At its January meeting in 1920, the commission decided to test the matter in court and directed the state attorney general "to establish the rights of the United States and of the State of Michigan in and to such reserved strip."

The decision to go to court was anything but impromptu. The Park Commission had received a $50,000 appropriation from the State Legislature to buy lake frontage between the Chippewa and Iroquois hotels, remove the buildings there, and make a park. The docks were to be purchased, too, and improved so they'd make an attractive entrance to the island. Many local businessmen, however, had major investments in buildings in the 100-foot zone, and others had been eyeing land there for new development. Prentiss Brown,

the St. Ignace lawyer who represented the property owners, was himself an investor in the Arnold Transit Company and had a lot at stake personally. The lawsuit dragged on through the 1920s and created a great deal of animosity between the Park Commission and the island's business community. After extensive action in state courts, the matter was referred to the U.S. Department of Justice and finally resolved in the early 1930s in favor of the people who claimed ownership of portions of the 100-foot reservation.

THE LARGEST PURCHASE OF land on Mackinac was from the Early family in 1923. The area, known technically as Private Claim #1 and by islanders as "the Early Farm," was the site of the Battle of 1814. It had originally been deeded by the U.S. Government to Michael Dousman in 1829. The cross-island road between the city and the British Landing at the island's north end ran through the middle of the farm. It was a private road where it crossed the farm, and a gate marked the boundary between private and public land.

Over the years a few small parcels had been sold for cottages, both on the east side of the property and in the British Landing area. A 440-acre parcel east of the road was owned by John Early who, in 1902, had leased to the park a 30-foot strip along the shore for construction of the Lake Shore Boulevard. The 172 acres west of British Landing Road were owned in the 1920s by the heirs of Peter Early, and a large portion of that land was leased to the Wawashkamo Golf Club.

The lands were offered to the state in order to

Arch Rock

be added to the park. After inspecting the lands the commission, on August 29, 1923, authorized the purchase of the 172 acres from Peter Early's estate for $25,000 and the 440 acres from John Early for $50,000.

It was at the same meeting that commissioners authorized buying part of the ill-fated, 36-acre Brown's Brook property mentioned earlier. They paid a man named Donald T. Mackinnon $1,600 for an undivided 30/63 interest in the tract and four years later bought another 13/63, but the land went undeveloped except for a picnic area the State Highway Department built near the mouth of the brook. After a later owner of the other 20/63 successfully laid claim to the whole thing in the 1970s, the courts left the state with only the small picnic area.

As the Twenties roared on, word got out that the Park Commission was interested in purchasing land, and in 1924 it was offered 30 acres between Annex and Harrisonville Roads, in a tract called Private Claim #4, immediately east of Hubbard's Annex. The parcel, which came as two undivided half interests, was the last major acreage purchased on the island, and since then only a number of buildings and small lots have been acquired.

On the mainland, the commission continued to acquire land for years. In the 1920s, Michilimackinac State Park was booming with campers and the commission decided to reconstruct the 18th-century fort there. Then it realized it did not own the whole site and part of the old fort was on land that was private. In 1925 the commission bought all of two city blocks, and Mackinaw City closed parts of Straits Avenue and DePeyster Street so that land, too, could be added to Michilimackinac State Park. Five years later part of another block was added.

Sometimes the commission acquired land it did not want. In 1923, a Donald T. Mackinnon gave the Park Commission 20 acres in St. Ignace for use as a public auto camp—the first of several efforts to get the commission to develop park land on the north side of the Straits. The commission accepted the 20 acres, but said it would develop an auto camp only if the State Legislature provided funds and the citizens of St. Ignace gave additional land between the Mackinnon parcel and the lake. This never happened, and the Park Commission subsequently gave the land to the Department of Conservation.

The commission was not philosophically limited to Mackinac Island and Mackinaw City, however. In 1924, it asked Congressman Frank D. Scott's help in getting title to Round Island from the U. S. Government. Scott succeeded, and on July 16, 1926, the 300-acre island—except for the lighthouse there—was deeded to the commission for park use. The commission was interested in Round Island because, unlike Mackinac Island, whose shore is mostly rock and gravel, it has a sand beach. It seemed a natural addition to the park, to provide a swimming area. The Park Commission never developed any facilities on Round Island, however, and the Federal Government secured its return in the 1930s as an addition to Hiawatha National Forest.

LEFT: The John Early farmhouse on the east side of British Landing Road.

BELOW: British Landing Road, site of the 1814 battle. Wawashkamo Golf course is on the left.

THE 20-PLUS YEARS of Frank Kenyon's superintendency, while memorable for prosperity and expansion, were not without rough spots, and they eventually led to his departure. A memorable rough spot came late in the 1920s when—heaven forbid—an automobile appeared on Mackinac Island. The chairman of the commission, Gustav A. Hendricks, happened to see it, and he angrily told Kenyon to tow the car away.

Hendricks, like Judge Wood a decade before, was keenly interested in history, and a driving force behind a revival of the historical aspects of the commission program. He proposed and supported commemorative celebrations as a way of getting federal funds, and was one of the early architects of what eventually became the restoration of Fort Mackinac.

One reason Hendricks was sensitive to the appearance of that automobile in 1927 had to do with the politics of the state and the commission. The year before, Kenyon had proposed a parking lot on the island where visitors could leave their cars. The idea upset a lot of people, and the governor had been flooded with complaints. Earlier in 1927, moreover, the State Legislature had passed a bill that bound commissioners closely to the politics of the moment by eliminating the members' fixed terms of office and providing that they serve, instead, at the pleasure of the governor.

A complete reorganization was clearly in the

Aerial views of Mackinac Island in 1939 and 1994. Note the outline of the Early Farm, the darker area at the top of the 1939 photograph. Compare the airports. The 1939 clearing east of Harrisonville was for a planned golf course. The recent Woods course shows in the 1994 photo.

offing. Now letters flowed into the office of newly elected Governor Fred W. Green, seeking this or that person's appointment as a commissioner.

With them came letters both supporting and opposing Superintendent Kenyon, whose job had always been year-to-year, and whose strong-willed leadership had made him a controversial figure on the island among both townspeople and influential cottagers. B. Frank Emery, the super-intendent Kenyon had replaced 18 years earli-er, even wrote to request his own reappointment.

Kenyon was someone people either respect-ed and liked a great deal, or did not care for at all. Robert H. Benjamin, the island postmaster, wrote on Kenyon's behalf: "A great majority of the people on Mackinac Island hope Mr. Keny-on will not be removed from here. He has done good work, always industrious, and carefully looking after the interests of the State and the public's welfare."

On the other hand the influential manager of Grand Hotel, William Stewart Woodfill, wrote: "Mr. Kenyon makes a good foreman, but is entire-ly incapable of developing the Island park, as evi-denced by his twenty years' experience here."

The new law created a rather awkward situa-tion during the summer of 1927, so the status quo got a brief respite. Plans were well underway for the National Governors' Conference on Mack-inac Island that July, and more than 20 gover-nors had already accepted Governor Green's invi-tation. The Governor, not wanting to rock the boat, asked the old commissioners to continue to function through the summer, saying he felt "that this is the biggest event that has come along

in recent years in which the Island and the Com-mission were involved."

That fall, three of the commissioners—Ira A. Adams, Burt D. Cady and Dana H. Hinkley—were reappointed. J. Walter Dohany of Detroit replaced the ailing John W. Fead, who died the following year.

Through the tense times, Superintendent Kenyon kept in close touch with Governor Green and worked hard at becoming what he called "pals in a common cause." Kenyon even sug-gested that Mackinac be made the Summer Cap-ital of Michigan. On June 8, 1928, Kenyon was reappointed superintendent for another year.

As things turned out, he lasted three years more—through the Crash of 1929 and the on-set of the hardest times yet. But his days were numbered.

BELOW: Starting in 1923 state-owned ferries regularly carried cars between St. Ignace and Mackinaw City.

mission "to make it very plain just exactly what the State proposes doing." Superintendent Kenyon replied that the plan was still tentative, and suggested that not all the complaints were motivated by objections to automobiles. "The local dock and steamboat interests," he said, "are not in sympathy with the State-owned ferry, or any other docks on Mackinac Island. They have had such a monopoly for so many years, that they cry out at the thought of any competition, or semblance of competition." Kenyon's suggestion was not unreasoned; when the Island Transportation Company reduced fares from 90 to 60 cents in 1926, the commission welcomed the thought of more visitors. Kenyon himself noted in his 1927 report that the old rates were "prohibitive to a poor man with a small family whom he wished to have see this beautiful public park."

Kenyon pressed on with his plan. His budget request for 1925-26 included $6,000 to construct a dock at British Landing and $10,000 to erect a 100-car garage there. Work on the docks began in 1926 and continued in 1927, but the garage was never built, and the project was a flop. State ferry service began on September 7, 1928, and ended December 7. Altogether, 727 passengers

arrived and 687 departed. Two cows and four horses made the crossing. No cars ever came. Otto Lang, CEO of the Arnold Transportation Company—not exactly a disinterested observer—felt that the primary users of the British Landing ferry were island "moonshiners" who were going to St. Ignace to purchase the grain and sugar they needed to make their hooch.

Service was not resumed in 1929. The dock, rebuilt in the 1970s, now serves for unloading material and equipment for State Park and local government public works projects.

No one knew at the outset, of course, that the project would fail, so the docking of the first car ferry made everyone nervous, and some people felt that the Island would be overrun by cars. That might explain the ruckus that erupted two days later, on the evening of September 9, 1928, when the chairman of the Park Commission, G. A. Hendricks, saw someone driving a car up Grand Hill from the downtown area to Harrisonville. Hendricks, on his way to catch the ferry for a trip to Grand Rapids, nearly exploded. According to a letter Kenyon later wrote a friend, when Hendricks reached the dock he threw out his chest and told Ted, the State Park carriage driver: "Locate Mr. Kenyon at once, tell him I said to locate that car at once, draw the gasoline from the tank, and tow it back to the dock with the State team and ship it off the Island OR WE WILL HAVE A NEW SUPERINTENDENT."

Hendricks, appointed to the commission only the year before, was particularly sensitive to his new position of responsibility. When he reached Grand Rapids on September 10, he immediately wired Superintendent Kenyon:

WIRE ME A COMPLETE CENSUS OF ALL AUTOMOBILES EITHER ANTIQUATED OR ABLE TO RUN UNDER THEIR OWN POWER OR BEARING LICENSE THAT MAY BE ON THE ISLAND. ALSO REMOVE ALL GASOLINE FROM THE TANKS OF AUTOMOBILES CAPABLE OF RUNNING WHETHER LICENSED OR NOT—ALSO DEPORT ALL CARS THAT MAY BE ON THE ISLAND OR IN STORAGE—NO CARS TO RUN UNDER THEIR OWN POWER—THEY MUST BE TOWED OVER THE SAME ROUTE AND NO OTHER THAT THEY ENTERED AND AT THE SAME TIME OF DAY—ALSO ASK THE COOPERATION OF THE ALGOMAH AND ARNOLD DOCK FOR COMPLETE TABULATION OF ALL POWERED VEHICLES. ALSO POSSIBLE ARRANGE THE TOWING BY STATE TEAMS AT A REASONABLE PRICE—USE ALL STATE EMPLOYEES IN TAKING CENSUS IF NECESSARY—CENSUS TO BE COMPLETED WITHIN TWENTY FOUR HOURS—ANSWER BY WIRE AND CONFIRM BY LETTER. —G. A. HENDRICKS

Kenyon found only three cars on Mackinac Island and none, he said, on state property. One was a hulk without an engine. The second was a Willys-Knight stored in a barn at Birch Lodge [Silver Birches] and the third car was at the home of William Smith in Harrisonville.

It was the third car which Hendricks had seen running up Grand Hill. Kenyon learned that Smith, a City Council member and a justice of the peace, had brought the car to the Island on the Algomah and landed it at the Arnold Dock. With permission from the mayor, he drove the car to his home to repair it. Kenyon also learned that the Arnold dock often stored cars for tourists who came to the Island on lake boats and that

cars were sometimes transferred between boats at the dock.

Kenyon did not draw off the gasoline or tow any of the cars he found, since none, he said, were on state property. Had he followed Hendricks' instructions, Kenyon reported, he "would be a trespasser upon private property" and guilty of "larceny of an automobile." Moreover, he said, "Our jurisdiction ends at the limits of the State Park property." Kenyon neglected to mention that a part of the road up Grand Hill is a State Park road.

THE ILL-FATED CAR PARK IDEA kept simmering into the 1930s when, during the Depression, attracting people to Mackinac Island was the name of the game. No one worked harder at it than Roger Andrews, managing editor of the *Detroit Times* and a member of the Park Commission for three two-year terms.

Andrews favored the car-park idea, but other commissioners were against it. In April, 1933, some island residents petitioned the commission to revive the project, but the commission's minutes show that the members voted later to "inform those interested that in view of the fact that the Commission does not have sums available for camp sites, policing, etc. that for the present the Commission is opposed to the landing of automobiles at British Landing, believing that with the present steamship ferry and aviation facilities, additional facilities for transportation will not be required for the season of 1934."

The matter of automobiles on the island was finally put to rest in 1935 when the Park Commission adopted a resolution saying "that the operation of any motor vehicle of any kind within the area of Mackinac Island State Park is hereby prohibited and that the Mackinac Island State Park Commission hereby adopts as a rule and regulation this restriction, and authorizes the Superintendent and any police officer to enforce by arrest and prosecution, the violation of this rule and regulation."

The rule kept the automobile at bay, and a year later Superintendent Clark R. Ladd reported: "The matter of automobiles on the Island, has, we feel, been settled definitely for all time. We made one arrest and obtained a conviction, both in Justice Court on the Island, and in Circuit Court at St. Ignace. In this connection, we publicized the trial as much as possible. In this way we kept the feature of the Island before the people at all times. We are more than pleased to report that since that time, we have not heard of a single violation of the no car rule."

Though the commission had established a rule prohibiting cars in the park, not until 1960 was the rule incorporated in state law, as an amendment to the 1927 act under which the Park Commission operates. With a few exceptions, the amendment forbids the commission from "permitting the use of motor vehicles" in the park. Aside from government and public utility vehicles, the only exception is that the commission may issue temporary permits for other vehicles to operate on park roads. That exception, as we'll see, proved important a few years later when the snowmobile came along.

The Snowmobile Exception

8

A FEW YEARS AFTER the legislature turned the Park Commission's rule against motor vehicles into state law, a new type of motor vehicle came along that threatened to change everything. It was the snowmobile, a machine that uniquely met the needs of year-round islanders.

Nearly every winter an "ice bridge" forms, across which people can travel between the island and St. Ignace. Brave islanders test the ice and mark the safe route with the carcasses of islanders' Christmas trees. In the early days, people would walk or ski across, and horses and dog sleds hauled freight. A few daredevils even drove autos across, and once, some islanders equipped a sled with an airplane engine and propeller to haul supplies.

Dr. Petersen's photograph of the 1969 protest parade.

When snowmobiles were developed, people found they were better suited to these tasks than anything. Besides, they were fun. Snowmobiles soon appeared on the island and its park roads.

There was nothing really new about motor vehicles on Mackinac. Government and utility vehicles had operated there for years, although it was not widely advertised. Plows have been used since 1947 to keep roads open for fire trucks, which were there before that. In the late 1940s trucks were used to spray insecticide, although only in the wee hours so visitors would not know. In the 1980s, there was no hiding the trucks and heavy equipment used during the two-year rebuilding of the island's sewer and water system.

The snowmobile's debut on the island was a bit more controversial. While islanders realized automobiles would ruin summer's horse-drawn carriage business, most had no objection to snowmobiles. Winter is when the 500 year-round residents "take back" their island from summer's hordes, and if islanders were to drive snowmobiles when there were no tourists to see them, what harm could it do?

The Park Commission did not see it that way. In April, 1968, concerned about snowmobilers' violations of the motor-vehicle ban, the commission officially "reaffirmed its obligation and intent to enforce the State Statute." The next September, the commission instructed Park Director Eugene T. Petersen to inform local authorities of the existence of this Statute.

These words fell on deaf ears. A few months later the Mackinac Island Snowmobile Club requested permits for snowmobile safaris in the State Park. Citing the new law, the commission denied the request. The island's snowmobilers, led by Mayor Otto "Bud" Emmons himself, paraded in protest in front of Marquette Park. Director Petersen documented the parade on film.

Local sentiment was so strong that the next September, the City Council adopted a resolution saying that "the controlled and restricted use of snowmobiles from December 15th to April 1st would be highly desirable and would not impair the tradition and image of Mackinac Island as a horse-drawn vehicle attraction center." The council requested that the Park Commission open a few park roads to snowmobiles.

At its October 23 meeting the commission

granted permits to residents of Harrisonville to use snowmobiles, but only on one road to the ice bridge at British Landing, and only between December 15, 1970, and April 1, 1971. (Park authorities also cited several people for alleged violations of the motor vehicle ban, but the prosecutor was not eager to press the cases, and they dragged on in court.) The next year the permit for Harrisonville residents was renewed, but on April 17, 1972, Judge Robert A. Wood ruled that it was discriminatory to issue permits to residents of Harrisonville only, and not to other islanders.

That being the case, the commission decided, no one would use snowmobiles. The next September the commission repealed its snowmobile resolution and instructed the director "to enforce the state law prohibiting the use of motorized vehicles within the State Park."

Not being able to use snowmobiles to reach the ice bridge, however, is a great inconvenience to islanders, and on November 3 the commission relented. It adopted a resolution authorizing December 15-April 1 permits for all island residents to use certain roads to reach British Landing, so they would have "winter access to the mainland for health, safety, education, and work convenience."

Over the years the list of designated roads has grown, but the Park Commission still re-adopts the resolution each year because of that state law requiring the permits to be temporary.

9 Hard Times

CCC crew
renovating the
West Blockhouse.

IN 1931, A YEAR AND A HALF AFTER the Crash of '29 touched off the Depression, the Mackinac Island State Park Commission underwent a major upheaval of its own. That year Governor Wilber M. Brucker, exercising a prerogative granted by the legislature, replaced the entire Park Commission.

What allowed him to do this was a statute in 1927 supplanting the law that had governed the Park Commission since 1895. The legislature had actually abolished the commission momentarily and established a new one, along with new provisions to govern it. One of the new provisions eliminated the commissioners' fixed terms of office. Now, commissioners would serve at the governor's pleasure.

The governor in 1927, Republican Fred W. Green, simply reappointed the same commission. But when Brucker was elected in 1930, he replaced all five members with new appointees—John Haggerty, Francis X. St. Peter, Thomas G. Bennett, Lee Smits and Kenneth M. Stevens. Under the new system, the politicization of the Park Commission was such that meetings were often held in the governor's office and commissions identified themselves by the name of the governor who had appointed them. In 1931, these five men were "Brucker's Commission." When they first met, in Lansing on May 5, 1931, Brucker himself called the meeting to order.

The members elected Haggerty chairman, and former commissioners Roger M. Andrews and G. A. Hendricks made reports to their successors. Then Hendricks recommended that Frank Kenyon be retained as superintendent.

The new commission voted, instead, to replace him, "effective immediately, but with pay continuing to June 30, 1931."

Waiting in the wings was Clarence La Chance, formerly mayor of Mackinac Island. Andrews introduced him to the commissioners and, after a brief interview, they appointed him superintendent, to begin immediately.

At its next meeting, on May 30 on the island, Kenyon met for a long time with the commission to ask them to give him the job of erecting the palisade for the reconstruction then underway at Fort Michilimackinac. Even that job was denied him. LaChance would handle it, they said, telling Kenyon to turn over all records. After 22 years as superintendent—and at the outset of the Depression—Frank Kenyon was out of a job.

Because of his passing, coupled with the replacement of the entire commission, much institutional memory was lost. For more than 20 years there had been a measure of continuity and direction on the commission. The 1930s, although punctuated by major accomplishments, were basically a time of administrative confusion. LaChance lasted but two years. Then a new governor, from a new party, named new commissioners who hired a new superintendent. For the rest of the tumultuous decade, commissioners and superintendents came and went at two-year intervals.

It would have been bad enough in prosperous times, but it was doubly difficult during the Depression, when the commission was forced to operate on meager resources. In the late 1920s, the legislature had been appropriating approxi-

LEFT: Unoccupied cottages on the West Bluff were shuttered for protection during the Depression.

BELOW: CCC crew completing the Eagle Scout barracks in 1934.

mately $40,000 a year for the park, plus funds for land purchases and construction. In 1931 the appropriation was reduced to $29,000, and then, in a statewide round of 15-percent cuts, to $24,650. In 1933, the appropriation was only $14,500. Like the rest of the country, the Mackinac Island State Parks learned to do with less.

The Depression, moreover, would persist on Mackinac through World War II. While defense spending was a boon to the national economy, wartime rationing and travel restrictions only tightened the lid on Mackinac. Worse, the military sucked up manpower, ending the New Deal public-works projects on the island.

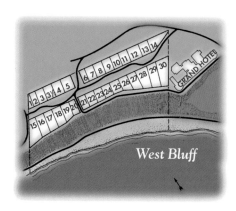

RIGHT: Map of State Park leases on the West Bluff.

Brochure advertising the 1934 Nicolet Tricentennial and the Historical Fair in an effort to lure tourists to Mackinac.

ONE OF THE BRIGHT THINGS about Depression-era Mackinac was Roger M. Andrews, managing editor of the *Detroit Times*, who had served briefly on the commission prior to the upheaval of 1931. Left off of "Brucker's Commission" in 1931, Andrews remained Mackinac's greatest booster nonetheless. In 1933, with the election of a new governor, he found himself back on the commission for two years, and in 1937-38 he served two more. In 1934-35 and 1937-38, he also served as an unpaid park superintendent, reviving a precedent from the earliest days when a commissioner doubled as superintendent during hard times. Through the Depression, whether a commissioner or not, he organized and promoted special events and historical fairs, developed and produced promotional brochures, authored reams of news releases, and edited a summer Mackinac Island newspaper called the *Mackinac Island News*. In 1938, he authored and published a popular book, *Old Fort Mackinac on the Hill of History*, and gave the copyright to the Park Commission.

On the day "Brucker's Commission" took over, Andrews urged them to use publicity and advertising to attract people to Mackinac. As a newspaper man, Colonel Andrews always had a sense of publicity, and from his first summer on the commission in 1929 he had pushed for a promotion campaign.

He had found a kindred spirit in Commissioner G. A. Hendricks, a Grand Rapids furniture-company president, with whom he spearheaded creation of the Mackinac Island Bureau. He got the commission to set up a State Park Press Bureau, whose single employee, Mr. Jean Worth, sent out weekly newsletters to papers.

Knowing the value of publicity, Andrews loved festivals. For the dedication of the newly reconstructed Fort Michilimackinac in 1933 he arranged a re-enactment of the 1763 Indian attack, establishing a tradition that continues today. The next event he engineered was an even bigger 1934 tricentennial celebration of the year Jean Nicolet became the first European to see the Straits. It kicked off the annual, summer-long Mackinac Island State Historical Fair at Old Fort Mackinac. Andrews was also a skilled fund-raiser; even in the Depression he raised $13,300 for the 1934 events, including $1,000 for prizes for such things as historical exhibits and needlework. Displays included a lacrosse stick said to have been used by an Ojibwa Indian at the capture of Michilimackinac in 1763, and a day book kept by the American Fur Company on Mackinac Island. As publicity, the fairs were rousing successes, and Andrews compiled two stout scrapbooks. Prizewinners included local residents named Alecia Poole, Blanche Fenton, Rose Van Allen Webster, Stella King and Nellie Donnelly, plus Mrs. William A. Comstock of Ann Arbor—whose husband just happened to be governor.

FOR ALL THESE PUBLICITY successes, the Park Commission frantically searched for new sources of revenue as the Depression deepened. In 1933, commissioners authorized a 25-cent nightly parking fee at the Mackinaw City campground, and a 10-cent admission charge at Fort Mackinac and at

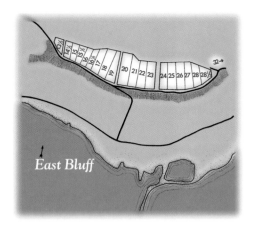

Michilimackinac State Park. The fees produced $4,036—a significant addition to the budget in those times—before being abolished in 1935.

Things would get so lean that Andrews would revive the old idea from 1897 of giving the park back to Uncle Sam. In the commission's 1937-1938 report, he wrote that if the state could not maintain its million-dollar investment, the fort should be given back. The National Park Service, he reported, was willing to restore Mackinac Island to National Park status if the Michigan Legislature concurred. Fortunately for Michigan, it never happened.

A major casualty of the Depression was a project begun in 1927 to expand Wawashkamo golf course and lay out new cottage sites adjacent to it. Reduced appropriations killed the golf course, and hard times killed demand for cottage sites, totally dashing any hope the commission had of raising additional revenue from new leases.

While the commission raised fees with one hand, it lowered them with the other, as lessees fell into default and, in some cases, boarded up unoccupied cottages. In 1933, the commission reduced fees 10 percent for anyone whose payments were not in arrears. To encourage occupancy, the commission offered another 15-percent discount on cottages that were occupied. It was not universally successful. In 1935 the commission sued 13 lessees to regain possession. Six owners brought their payments up to date, but two sold out, and the rest faced foreclosure.

One lessee who appeared before the commission to protest the foreclosure was Mrs. Matella Eckhart, who had purchased a house on lot 28½ of the East Bluff in 1926. Mrs. Eckhart said emphatically that, for sentimental reasons, she would not give it up. As the commission's minutes reveal, she explained that "she was blessed with second sight, and that when she first saw the house, she could see her father on the porch." The bewildered commission referred her case to the attorney general, but eventually negotiated a settlement that let her stay.

Five cottages reverted into the hands of the state for non-payment of taxes. After the Park Commission began a program of maintaining them, Superintendent Clark R. Ladd reported in 1936 that it "made the whole Island take on a more prosperous aspect." He added that "The summer houses, which were run down and deserted and a sure indication of the loss of prestige of this Island among the better summer resorts of America, now indicate a return to the day when Mackinac Island will once more be considered among the world's finest."

The return was not swift, however, and in the meantime the Park Commission not only had to maintain cottages it did not want but also had to live without the income from leasing them. Commissioners put the repossessed East Bluff cottages up for sale, at fire-sale prices. They asked $2,000 for the Pridmore house on Lot 13½, and $1,500 for the Schantz cottage Lot 16. The price on the Gillespies' place on Lot 23 was $2,500, and the Hamilton house on Lot 27 could have been bought for only $300 by anyone who would spend $1,000 on repairs within six months. Two of the houses quickly sold. The O'Neil house, on Lot 25, was priced at $2,000 and went unsold until

1941, when it fetched only $750. The cottage on Lot 13½ on the East Bluff remained unsold until 1946, when an Alan Sawyer paid $1,000—$250 down and annual installments of $100.

To attract and keep lessees the commission slashed rents again in 1939 by 60 percent to anyone whose back fees were paid, and quit renting apartments in the fort to avoid competing with private rentals elsewhere on the island. In 1942, fees were halved again, and the commission reduced concessionaires' fees, hoping to keep them in business. Fees fell to a $1 a year in the cases of the Grand Hotel and Wawashkamo golf courses and the Fort Mackinac tea room and Mary B. Loud's Block Printing concession in the fort. The annual fee for the Arch Rock concession was reduced to only $100. With so little revenue from park activities, nearly all park funds in those dark days came from state appropriations.

Depression-era fee reductions marked a shift in the rationale behind park-land leases. From the time the park had been created by the Federal government, leases had been a major revenue source. Now they were viewed as a way simply to keep properties occupied and looking well.

Before World War II ended, Mackinac Island was in such a depressed state that even many of the shops on Main Street were empty. To keep up at least an appearance of prosperity, the Arnold Transportation Company, a principal property owner on Main Street, required tenants to display merchandise in the windows of empty stores.

The issue of how to handle tax-reverted lands on Mackinac Island had become acute by 1940. The most significant tax-reverted property was the Island House Hotel, which became state property in 1941. The state leased it the next year to an international religious and political organization called "Moral Re-Armament," which used it as a conference center. Until 1948, the Island House was a center of controversy as title to it changed hands among the Department of Conservation, the City of Mackinac Island, and the Park Commission.

The old hotel's status became a hot political issue in 1946. MRA brought about 3,000 people to Mackinac each summer to what it called its "training center for strengthening democracy and building sound labor-management relations." The attendees helped extend the usual July-August summer season because they were on the island from early June to mid-November. And, since MRA employed islanders and used local services, island residents welcomed them and hoped they'd continue coming to the Island. In March, 1946, in fact, many island voters signed a petition urging that MRA "be encouraged to maintain their summer headquarters here."

In 1946, the Department of Conservation deeded the Island House to the Park Commission, which then had to choose between continuing to lease the hotel to MRA or seek someone to operate it as a hotel. MRA stayed on through 1947, while the property went back and forth again between the Department of Conservation and the Park Commission. Finally, in 1948, the MRA asked for a 10-year, rent-free lease, the Park Commission refused, and the Island House was once again leased for use as a hotel.

By 1944, when the state appropriation was

Finely carved wooden markers were made by WPA artists for the Island's historic buildings.

only $29,400, the commission was too poor even to monitor the Mackinac Island deer park. Turned loose, the deer were soon wiped out by dogs and hunters.

DESPITE ALL THIS GLOOM, the Depression also brought accomplishments in the parks. Federal relief money and programs came to the island, and such New Deal "alphabet" agencies as the CCC, CWA, ERW and WPA did a tremendous amount of work.

The CCC—Civilian Conservation Corps— had a camp in the State Park all but one year from 1933 to 1938. Its crews erected a number of buildings in the middle of the Island on the former Early Farm east of British Landing Road. Men from the camp cleared brush along roads and trails to help prevent forest fires, and worked on landscaping projects at the Military Cemetery and other scenic island spots.

During 1934 the CCC crew undertook extensive repairs to the historic buildings at Fort Mackinac, and when fire destroyed the old Fort Holmes blockhouse in the early 1930s, the CCC crews rebuilt it. In 1935 the park received a grant of $17,394 for an accurate reconstruction of all of Fort Holmes. Following detailed plans revealed by historical research and using wood cut on the island, the park crew reconstructed the fort under the direction of Fort Michilimackinac Manager Chris Schneider. The reconstructed fort was dedicated on July 11, 1936.

One of the most significant projects undertaken by the Park Commission during the Depression was the reconstruction of Fort Michilimackinac. Conceived at the end of Kenyon's superintendency but halted by political and economic upheavals, the job resumed in 1931 and was finished in 1933.

Even during World War II, the Park Commission managed to undertake some significant projects. At its December 7, 1943, meeting the commission accepted the Early House (now Beaumont Memorial) as a gift from the Parke, Davis Company, along with the company's pledge of $5,000 to help restore it. The commission also acquired by gift the Biddle House, the oldest surviving residential structure on Mackinac Island. It was years before either was fully restored, but the acquisitions marked the start of new focus on historic properties and the challenge of restoring them.

ROGER ANDREWS WAS NOT THE only person interested in promoting Mackinac Island in the 1930s. In 1935 former Republican Senator Wilfird F. Doyle presented to the commission a plan for getting greater publicity and exposure for the island. The year before, with a Democratic governor's commission in office, Doyle had made a name for himself by alleging "intolerable conditions" and wrongdoing on Mackinac Island and calling for an investigation. Now, with a Republican commission appointed, Doyle offered to work with them in lobbying for state funds with which to advertise.

Thus, W. F. Doyle began a long and involved association with the Mackinac Island State Park Commission which lasted for more than 50 years.

RIGHT: Federal funds paid for new water and steam heating lines at Fort Mackinac.

BELOW: CCC camp on the former Early Farm.

Andrews and Doyle had much in common. Both hailed from Menominee, in the Upper Peninsula, where they had been political rivals. Not exactly a team, they nonetheless had the island's interests equally at heart. Through most of the Depression and into the 1940s, Doyle the Republican and Andrews the Democrat were like an alternating current of electricity that powered the State Park through difficult times.

In his lobbying efforts to boost promotions, Doyle enlisted the aid of W. S. Woodfill, owner of Grand Hotel, and Otto Lang, head of the Arnold Transportation Company. He soon reported success: Contacts had been made for advertising in a number of papers and magazines, and the State Highway Department agreed to erect 200 signs advertising Mackinac Island which said, "Mackinac Island Straight Through."

A publicity brochure had been designed, and the islanders now persuaded the Highway Department to let the Park Commission build road-side information booths in St. Ignace and Mackinaw City. The booths were designed to look like blockhouses, and remained in use for many years. One still serves as the ticket booth at the Arnold dock in St. Ignace.

In 1937 a new Democratic Governor, Frank Murphy, appointed his own commission, again including Andrews. He became not only chairman but superintendent as well, because the park could not afford to hire anyone. The only perquisite he acquired was a single driving horse purchased for his use in driving around the park.

In 1939 the Republicans took back the governorship with Frank Fitzgerald, and when he made his appointments to the commission, he rewarded Doyle with appointment. Doyle was to remain a force in commission affairs for years, whether on or off the commission. Doyle, a man of remarkable charm and boundless energy, wanted to be in control. A master lobbyist and backstage manipulator with a forceful personality, he made himself, in a way, into the "King of the Island." When he needed ammunition for whatever scheme he was proposing, he assiduously researched commission minutes for precedents and searched law books for loopholes. He could out-argue and out-bluff the most astute politicians, and loved to depict himself as an Irish leprechaun. When he spouted his "Mackinac malarkey" tales, it was hard to separate fact from fiction. One of his favorite ploys was to deliberately confuse issues, and then charge in to save the day. He was known affectionately as "Foxy" Doyle.

Doyle, however, like Andrews, always believed

that the commission should be a "working" commission, involved in day-to-day administration as well as policy setting. Accordingly, in December, 1939, soon after Doyle became a commissioner, the commission agreed unanimously "that not less than three Commissioners [should] be present at Mackinac Island during as much of the summer season as seems possible" because "sufficient matters of importance present themselves during the summer to have a majority of the Commissioners available for special meetings without incurring additional State expense." And of course, if commissioners were to be on Mackinac all summer they would need quarters nicer than the public housing provided for occasional meetings. It is hard, after more than half a century, to be certain of Doyle's motives, but surely he expected to be one of those present in summer. As a lobbyist, Doyle was busy elsewhere when the legislature was in session, but during the summer he had time available. And what better location to entertain his clients than beautiful Mackinac Island?

Doyle put down firm roots in 1940 when he purchased his own cottage on lot 14-1/2 of the East Bluff and Mackinac Island became his legal residence. The next year he worked through the legislature a bill adding a sixth member to the commission and requiring that it be a resident of the island. From there, it was only a short step to have himself appointed by Republican Governor Luren Dickinson.

The same new law, however, also gave commissioners the fixed, six-year terms of office they enjoy today. Newly elected governors could no longer name entirely new members, and later that year when Democrat Murray D. Van Wagoner became governor, Doyle the Republican stayed on.

World War II brought new opportunities to Doyle, if not to the park. Depression and war had left the commission almost entirely dependent on legislative appropriations, and Doyle, the master lobbyist, was in the driver's seat. On December 8, 1942, he was not just a commissioner, but was elected chairman of the Park Commission. No longer only a power behind the throne, he had become king.

By then, his old rival Roger Andrews was no longer a commissioner but was living on the island and editing the Mackinac Island News Magazine. Earlier in 1942, Andrews had asked the commission to give him housing quarters at Fort Mackinac in exchange for his writing news stories about the park. Doyle knew he and Andrews were too much alike and felt uncomfortable with Andrews closely involved in commission affairs. He argued against Andrews' request. But the commission granted it over Doyle's objection.

The next year, however, after Doyle became chairman, it was a different story. When Andrews asked for the quarters again that summer, the answer was, "No."

Doyle encouraged murky arrangements which gave him room to maneuver. While he headed the Park Commission, the line between city and state affairs on Mackinac was often fuzzy and imprecise, with much overlap between the park,

Highway sign from the 1930s encouraged motorists to visit Mackinac Island.

BELOW: Aerial view shows sails drying after a yacht race and a large cruise boat tied up at the Arnold Dock.

Commission in 1941, its president was Otto Lang, the CEO of Arnold Transportation Co., and among the members were W. Stewart Woodfill, owner of Grand Hotel, and—of course—"Bill" Doyle. When the city bought and restored the historic Robert Stuart House, the Park Commission loaned historic objects for display there.

The City of Mackinac Island's Park and Harbor Commission was created as a way to fund civic improvements in the face of the depressed economy. The commission was authorized to sell $250,000 in revenue bonds, which would be repaid with what amounted to a 25-cent head tax on each visitor to the island. Such a tax, however, was illegal, so some creative subterfuges were devised. The boat lines simply added the 25-cent charge to their fares and voluntarily paid the fee to the city. To get the Arnold Dock renovated, the city bought it for $7,000, refurbished it with bond money, and sold it back for $7,000. While the city owned it, Arnold leased the dock for a fee that, not surprisingly, came to about 25 cents for each visitor expected to disembark there. Since other lines used the dock, too, Arnold charged them wharfage on the same basis. The bonds were paid off on time, in 1956, and no investor ever complained.

Among the harbor projects was one in which sand dredged from the lake bottom was pumped ashore in a layer five feet thick at the end of the boardwalk below the West Bluff, forming a sand beach. Most of the sand has washed away, but a little remains, and islanders still use the area for sunbathing and still call it "the sand beach."

Hollyhocks were also planted on the Fort

the city, and other major players.

Doyle kept a hand in local politics, too. When park Superintendent C. R. Ladd resigned, Doyle was instrumental in naming as his replacement Robert Doud, a man active in local politics, and a former Mackinac Island mayor from an old island family. (At the same time the commission hired as dockmaster a man named Carl A. Nordberg, who, as things turned out, would succeed Doud four years later and remain as superintendent for 22 years.)

When the city formed a Park and Harbor

LEFT: The filming of "This Time for Keeps" is still talked about at Mackinac fifty years later.

Mackinac hillside and a shuffleboard court was constructed on the Marquette Park waterfront. Improvements in the harbor area had actually begun long before 1941. In 1929 and 1930, demand for small-boat moorings was so strong that Superintendent Kenyon had spent $10,000 expanding the yacht dock in the harbor, and had built a concrete sea wall and sidewalk there. In 1938, the Mackinac Island Yacht Club moved into the former Sweeney house west of the Island House Hotel, and leased a small dock opposite it from the park.

"BILL" DOYLE DID NOT BELIEVE in having many commission meetings. Two a year sufficed from 1943 through 1946. Between meetings, Doyle ran the commission's affairs pretty much as he pleased. Nor did Doyle concern himself much with paperwork or financial statements. On October 4, 1943, his annual report to Governor Harry F. Kelly stated:

"I doubt if any Governor has ever taken the time to read any of the reports which have been submitted in the past. Therefore, the following, in brief form.

"The Commission has submitted monthly reports of its financial structure to the Auditor General. The Auditor General has audited the books and accounts on regular schedules.

"The Commission has performed all of the duties imposed by law, has complied with all rules and regulations of state government, has adhered strictly to the letter of the civil service law and has devoted its time and energies in a sincere manner to maintain, manage and improve Macki-

nac Island State Park in the best possible interests of the taxpayers of Michigan."

The 1944 report was even shorter.

Doyle was equally cavalier in keeping park and city business separate. It often happened over the years that the line grew fuzzy between city and state when it came to looking after island affairs. Doyle's main concern was always the island, and he seldom concerned himself with whether a particular job that needed doing was properly the city's or the park's. It was all one to him. In 1956 he obtained a $9,000 appropriation to run half a mile of city water main to Harrisonville, and no one worried that park crews spent six weeks working on the project to keep it within budget.

IN LATE 1944, DOYLE HELPED the Park Commission forge an even closer relationship with the governor's office that lasts to this day. It so happened that Governor Kelly was planning to host a national conference of governors on Mackinac Island the next summer, and Doyle sniffed opportunity.

Since 1935, the governor had had a modest island residence, but for the conference, Doyle decided, something better was in order. One of the leased properties which had fallen on hard times during the Depression was the large cottage built in 1902 by Lawrence A. Young on the knoll immediately west of Fort Mackinac. Young had spent $15,000 to build it, and in 1944 the cottage's new owner, Hugo Scherer, had it on the market at the same price.

With his considerable lobbying skills, Doyle

managed to have $15,000 inserted into a park appropriation bill to purchase property on Mackinac Island, and used it to buy the run-down house, for the governor to use as his residence during the conference.

Then Doyle really got creative. Since the commission had no funds to renovate the house, Doyle turned to a source of free labor: prison inmates. Despite considerable local opposition, he had a crew of inmates brought to the island and housed in the Scout Barracks while they worked at making the old house liveable.

They finished in time for the governors' conference. During the renovation they painted the exterior of the house white, which was a marked contrast from its formerly dark stain. The final work was under the direction of Carl A. Nordberg, who replaced Robert Doud as Superintendent on July 1, 1945.

Despite his successes, Doyle was facing something of a crisis: His term on the commission was due to expire in April, 1947, and to win re-appointment, he knew, he needed help. He especially needed the mayor's help, because he was the resident commissioner, and the law that established the job also stipulated that the resident commissioner had to be nominated by the mayor. In his effort to curry favor with local officials, Doyle even engineered a bill authorizing the Park Commission to turn over Island House revenues to the local government.

There was always chronic friction between park and town, but Doyle also had problems of his own making in the local community. In the summer of 1946, when the Jimmy Durante-Esther Williams movie, "This Time for Keeps," was being filmed at Grand Hotel, Doyle had made a nuisance of himself. Such a nuisance, in fact, that hotel owner W. Stewart Woodfill had barred him from the hotel.

For support in renomination, Doyle was also counting on the island carriagemen, whose association was being threatened at the time with tough new controls. Doyle had close contacts with its leaders and worked closely with some of the 23 families, notably Alex Gillespie and Arthur Chambers, on incorporating a new organization, Mackinac Island Carriage Tours, and he drafted enabling legislation that would let the Park Commission grant the group a 30-year transportation franchise on the island. Not all the carriage men were in favor of the plan, but they were kept in the dark. The leaders favored the new arrangement, and it was they whose support Doyle needed.

In the end, Doyle's machinations failed him and the new Mayor of Mackinac Island, Alan Sawyer, nominated James F. Cable, owner of the Lake View Hotel, to be resident commissioner. Doyle was off the commission, but not for long. By April, 1948, he had wangled re-appointment. He paid his debts, too: One of the commission's acts at Doyle's first meeting following reappointment was to approve the 30-year franchise to Mackinac Island Carriage Tours.

When the popular G. Mennen Williams, a Democrat, took office as governor in 1948, he seemed likely to stay in office a while, and Doyle's days as a commissioner were numbered. Still, he managed to hold on another six years, and even

OPPOSITE PAGE: The Lawrence A. Young family of Chicago in front of their cottage.

LEFT: The Lawrence A. Young cottage. It was painted white in 1945 when it was acquired for use as the Governor's Summer Residence.

BELOW. Aerial view, 1937.

when he was no longer a commissioner, he played a role on the island. At one point in the late 1950s, as we'll see, that role would turn out to be vital to the future of the park.

10 Postwar Renaissance

Maggie and
Jiggs at
Michilimackinac.

MACKINAC ISLAND'S ECONOMY remained slow in the first few postwar years, but by the late 1940s things had begun to improve immensely. Gasoline was again plentiful, new cars rolled off assembly lines, and Americans were taking to the road in droves. Many headed for the Straits. In 1949, visitors to the Mackinaw City Trailer Camp numbered 128,000, a record. The $4,652 they paid in fees was the largest item in the park's $8,545 of earned revenue.

Until he died in 1952, Michilimackinac Park Manager Chris Schneider ran the park much as he had since 1921. Known affectionately as "The Buffalo Bill of the Mackinac Country," Schneider watched over his campers and the park's little zoo with equal care. The zoo had two black bears, named Maggie and Jiggs after the comic-page characters, as well as owls, bobcats, a raccoon, a fox and 100 doves. The fox was tame and followed the park's workers around like a dog. Inside the fort Harry J. Teysen managed a small museum and concession building; only later did he move the operation out of the park and into town. When Schneider died in 1952, his son, Reynolds "Red" Schneider, took over as Mackinaw City park manager.

Despite increasing attendance Michilimackinac remained a sideline for the Park Commission, which focused nearly all its attention on the island instead.

By war's end, the Mackinac Island park was officially under the day-to-day management of Carl Nordberg, but his wife, Katie, did all the paperwork, and some say it was she who actually ran the park. Carl would listen to the commissioners' wishes and give assignments each morning to the park crew and then, often as not, go off to play golf with the commissioners. Sometimes, he golfed with the governor as well.

After the uncertainty of the Depression years, when there was a new superintendent almost every other year, Nordberg brought stability back to the park. He served 22 years—the same as Frank Kenyon, although he never had the influence Kenyon had.

Nordberg, who had been a high school coach, loved young people and took special interest in the Eagle Scout program. He lived year-round at the superintendent's residence in Fort Mackinac and spent winters supervising the ice harvest in the harbor, or in the woods clearing dead timber and bringing in logs—for firewood or to be sawn as lumber in the mill. In spring and fall he and his crew focused on road maintenance. The park's roads had not yet been paved, and had to be graded, clayed, graveled and oiled. Erosion on the beach road was of continuing concern, too, and not long after the war, Fairy Arch and Scott's Cave were dynamited in a misguided effort to obtain rock for road repair and shoreline riprap.

It took a long time for the park to get up to speed in the postwar world, but when things started to move, they moved fast, and there were big things to come.

GMENNEN "SOAPY" WILLIAMS had played an active role in Park Commission affairs from the time he became governor in 1949. At the August 20 meeting that

LEFT: Harvesting ice at Mackinac was an annual activity until the 1950s.

BELOW: Governor G. Mennen Williams inspects Marty Petersen, the first guide at restored Fort Mackinac.

year, in the Governor's Summer Residence on the island, he made the first recorded motion by a governor as an ex-officio member of the Commission. It came as he locked horns with Park Commission Chairman W. F. Doyle.

As usual, when Doyle was involved, politics and showmanship played leading roles. At issue was Governor Williams' intent to name one of his new appointees as Park Commission chairman. Doyle had other ideas, and arrived girded

Reynolds Schneider supervised the popular camp ground at Michilimackinac.

for battle. As one colleague later wrote in his memoirs, "The Republican members led by Doyle and all dressed in white suits with Panama hats and walking sticks arrived at the Governor's porch one minute before starting time and the meeting got underway."

Doyle won the first skirmish when, after a 3-3 vote, he simply ruled that in the event of a tie the old chairman would continue.

At a subsequent meeting, when the commission again split 3-3 along party lines on electing a secretary, Governor Williams took advantage of his status as an ex-officio member and cast the deciding vote for Democrat Margaret Price, the first woman commissioner.

Chairman Doyle refused to announce the outcome of the election until he obtained legal advice as to the "eligibility of the Governor to vote as an Ex-Officio member." He said he would ask the Attorney General for a formal opinion, and that in the meantime Commissioner Edward A. Ward would serve as acting secretary. Doyle never got a ruling from the Attorney General, but wrote a lengthy brief of his own in which he determined that Governor Williams, "the member ex-officio, did not possess the right to vote."

Doyle left himself an out, however. In the minutes of that meeting, he is quoted as saying: "If the Chair is in error in this ruling, he will be among the first to cooperate to the end that the error may be corrected by the adjudication of the Supreme Court of Michigan."

Governor Williams did not forget the insult, and when Doyle's term was up, he would not be reappointed. But the governor had to wait even for that, since Doyle's term did not end until 1956, and during most of that time Doyle continued as chairman. Williams, a Democrat, was a popular governor, but Doyle was not without clout of his own. Republicans controlled the legislature, where Doyle, the Republican and master lobbyist, had considerable influence.

Politics did not vanish when it came time to choose a chairman in 1951. The candidates were Doyle and James P. Dunnigan, a Democrat newly named to the commission by Williams. The commission split 3-3 again, on party lines, but Doyle had already ruled, as chairman, that in the event of a tie the chairman would continue in office. Dunnigan was elected vice chairman.

It was the perfect beginning of a long, love-hate relationship between two Irishmen from opposing parties. Doyle and Dunnigan argued

THE SCOUTS

I N 1929, newly-appointed park Commissioner Roger Andrews organized a contingent of Eagle Scouts to serve as guides at Fort Mackinac. The program continues today as the Mackinac Island Scout Service Camp. The Scouts bunked in the former Fort Commissary building until 1934, when the Civilian Conservation Corps built them a barracks. The program lapsed for a few years but Andrews revived it in 1937 with financial support from Commissioner Lawrence Fisher. In the 1940s, Park Superintendent Carl Nordberg encouraged development of the scout program, which was no longer for Eagle Scouts alone. He turned the scheduling over to the Detroit Area Boy Scout Council, which continues to have a special interest. One Detroit troop—Troop 194—has participated 53 consecutive years. Girl Scouts, added to the program in 1974, make up about half the participants. Each year, about 600 scouts spend a week apiece on Mackinac, providing information to visitors, helping with park clean-up, and tending to park flags. The most illustrious scout was one the very first year who grew up to be president—a young man from Grand Rapids named Gerald R. Ford. President Ford's return in the summer of 1975 as guest of Governor William Milliken turned the island upside down. Secret Service agents spent a week setting up security, and Navy frogmen checked out a possible swimming site. The armored presidential limousine was secretly ferried out and hidden near Fort Mackinac. The president helicoptered in at 11:35 p.m. on a Saturday and spent the night at the Executive Summer Residence. Next day, after church, President Ford unexpectedly announced he was going downtown to buy fudge. That done, he decided to visit Fort Mackinac, where he pointed out to Park Superintendent Eugene T. Petersen where he had slept in the Commissary as a scout.

1938 Camp Murphy
OF THE GOVERNOR'S HONOR GUARD

Michigan Eagle Scouts Will Conduct You Through Old Fort Mackinac

This service is both gratuitous and informative. Scouts accept no fees. Rendering every possible service as Fort and Museum guides and guards.

Sponsored by M. I. State Park Commission

Commissioner Doyle alighting from Carriage Tours' "surrey with the fringe on top.,"

summer home, and after leaving office in 1960, bought the most impressive cottage on the West Bluff. When he died, he was buried on the island, his remains carried by horse-drawn hearse to the Protestant Cemetery. He is the state's only governor buried on Mackinac.

One of the things Governor Williams liked about the island was its marvelous history. It took him a while, however, to persuade Commissioner Doyle and the rest of the Park Commission that they, too, should pay history more heed.

ECHOES OF WARTIME had faded completely by the mid-1950s, and summer's crowds on Mackinac were growing year by year. By 1954, plans were well underway in Lansing for a $100 million project that would forever change the entire Straits—the Mackinac Bridge. The new highway it would carry, I-75, would reduce the drive to Mackinac from downstate to but four hours. The bridge would itself become a tourist attraction. Surely thousands more visitors would come each month to the Straits of Mackinac.

While the Park Commission paid scant attention to the historic value of its properties in the first few postwar years, there were signs of change. Much of the interest in the mid-Fifties stemmed from the interest and leadership of Margaret Price, the first woman on the commission. While the Beaumont Memorial's reopening in 1954 followed restoration by private benefactors, the commission had hired an expert from the Kalamazoo Public Museum to catalog the Fort Mackinac collection. Also in 1954, the com-

often over the years, but they had much in common, too, and often supported each other on Park Commission issues. Dunnigan succeeded Doyle as chairman in 1953, serving in that role until 1957, and remained continuously on the Park Commission until 1981. But Doyle returned to the commission in 1961 and remained a member until 1985. So firmly entrenched was Doyle, even when he finally retired, that he would not agree to step down unless he was feted at a farewell party in the Governor's Summer Residence. Dunnigan, like Doyle, put down roots on the island. He purchased the cottage on Lot 17 of the East Bluff, from where he could look out over the town and harbor and keep an eye on his boat moored in the marina.

These major players may have had opposing politics, but they all loved Mackinac Island. Governor Williams and his wife, Nancy, made it their

The beginning of big changes: Interstate 75 and the Mackinac Bridge with Michilimackinac State Park in the foreground.

mission acquired Michigan's oldest church—Old Mission Church, built in 1829—as a gift from its trustees.

In 1955 Governor Williams started to prod the commission into a greater role in historic preservation. He invited people who were involved in historical affairs around the state to a meeting that November 22 in Detroit to discuss the future of history at Mackinac.

It was a blue-ribbon group. All the commissioners were there except Chairman Dunnigan, who was ill. So were Dr. Lewis Beeson, executive secretary of the Michigan Historical Commission, and Professor Lewis VanderVelde of the University of Michigan, the primary authority on Michigan History. Professor Emil Lorch, the architect who had recently restored the Beaumont Memorial, attended. Mackinac Island Mayor Sam McIntire was there with other prominent islanders, and there were representatives

from the Attorney General's Office, Department of Conservation, and Michigan Tourist Council. They talked mainly of what to do about the crumbling Clerks' Quarters on Market Street, but discussion ranged, as well, to a restoration of Fort Michilimackinac and of sites in St. Ignace.

Although the group agreed to meet again, it never did. The governor, however, had planted a seed. When the park commissioners met the next month, they continued discussing the subject of historic restoration, and a significant idea surfaced for a way to finance the kinds of projects they were discussing. It is reflected in the minutes only as a discussion of "the advisability of creating a new Park and Harbor Authority when the present one expires, for the purpose of bonding for a rehabilitation program." But it turned out to be a very big idea.

The seed was beginning to germinate, but the ground was not yet fertile enough. That was made clear in 1956, when the Michigan Historical Commission approached the Park Commission about places in the park it might include in its new program to mark historical sites around the state. The commission, always jealous of its authority and stature, was wary of even that innocuous request. Its minutes reflect members' objections to any sign that "eliminated the fact that the property was part of, and under the jurisdiction of, The Mackinac Island State Park Commission."

When the Michigan State Medical Society complained about the commission's neglect of the recently renovated Beaumont Memorial, Governor Williams began to grow very impa-

RIGHT: The vine covered Biddle House awaiting restoration.

tient. In December, he wrote to urge greater " consideration by the Commission of the historical values of the island" and to suggest another meeting on the matter.

In reply, the minutes show, "The commission expressed the feeling that they would be glad to attend and cooperate with other agencies." They were really more interested, however, in overseeing the operations of Mackinac Island Carriage Tours and the Edison Sault Company's extension of high-voltage lines through the woods from Grand Hotel to Stonecliffe.

Governor Williams knew that if he wanted something to happen with historic development on Mackinac Island he had to find someone who would get the job done. From his summers on Mackinac, he knew that one of the most energetic and powerful men was W. Stewart Woodfill, owner of Grand Hotel. Woodfill had not only brought Grand Hotel successfully through the troughs of the Depression, he had been actively involved in civic affairs as a member of the island's Park and Harbor Commission.

With Woodfill as a commissioner, Williams decided, things might happen. Woodfill did not seek appointment (unlike most commissioners) so he was able to bargain when the governor approached him in 1957. To do the job, Woodfill said, he would have to be chairman. Agreed.

While Governor Williams was figuring out how to talk James Dunnigan into stepping down so Woodfill could replace him, Woodfill spent the early summer getting the lay of the land. He hosted a meeting at his home of the Michigan Historical Commission, and another at Grand Hotel of the Michigan Medical Society. Woodfill learned of the Historical Commission's concern for the restoration of the Clerks' Quarters, the Biddle House and Fort Mackinac, as well as for the architectural character of Main Street, and of its interest in reconstructing Fort DeBuade in St. Ignace.

He also heard the Historical Commission recommend moving the Mackinaw City trailer park out of town to make room for archaeological excavation and an authentic restoration of Fort Michilimackinac. Conversations at these meetings were detailed to the point of Woodfill's suggesting the use of prison labor, since it would be hard to get funds from the legislature for restoring historic sites.

The governor's emissary, John Abernathy reported back that Woodfill was getting the ball rolling. The next day Woodfill heard of the Medical Society's dissatisfaction over the Beaumont Memorial, which the commission had not even formally accepted following its restoration. Plans were made to fix a leaking rear wall and to properly accept and commemorate the restoration.

Meanwhile Governor Williams was greasing the ways for Woodfill's election as chairman at the commission's August 12, 1957, meeting. First the commission would revise a long-standing procedure that the chairman was always of the same party as the governor. Then Chairman Dunnigan resigned, citing "the demands of my personal business," and moved W. Stewart Woodfill's election as Chairman. It was unanimous.

The commission now had a tornado at its helm with the firm support of the governor. But, it had

BELOW: W. Stewart Woodfill in great
form showing Mrs. Lyndon Johnson
around Fort Mackinac in 1964.

no money. Woodfill's idea of using prison labor met with strong opposition from local residents, who remembered the boisterous prisoners who worked on the Governor's House in 1945. The legislature rebuffed Woodfill's request for a $500,000 appropriation.

Woodfill, not easily deterred, decided to get the money the old-fashioned way, by earning it. Since that took time, and he needed the cash up front, he knew from his business experience that he'd have to borrow it. The answer, he realized, lay in revenue bonds, like the ones the state had

RIGHT: Cal Peters at work on one of his intricate dioramas.

Turnstile token. Admission fees made possible the restoration of Fort Mackinac.

used for the Mackinac Bridge and the Mackinac Island Park and Harbor Commission had used back in 1941 for improvements on the island.

Revenue bonds, however, require revenue with which to repay them. How would restored forts earn money? Woodfill had that answer, too. He knew that several hundred thousand visitors came to Mackinac each year and that more than 100,000 of them trudged up the 150-foot hill to see the decrepit, old Fort Mackinac. If the fort were cleaned up and filled with interesting exhibits and displays, Woodfill reasoned, people would be willing to pay a modest fee to visit there and enjoy the superb, panoramic view of the Straits of Mackinac.

It was a good plan, but there was one more obstacle: Before the Park Commission could sell bonds, it had to have the State Legislature's authority to do so. Woodfill had his personal attorney draft the appropriate bill, and then, to guide the bill through the legislature, he turned to an old friend of the island's, former Commissioner W. F. "Bill" Doyle.

Woodfill and Doyle had crossed swords often, but both also knew when they needed each other, and this was one of those times. Doyle knew the workings of Lansing like no one else, and Woodfill held the keys to the fine life at Mackinac. Within a few months, early in 1958, Bill 201 lay on Governor Williams' desk awaiting his signature.

It was a sweeping mandate. It would give the Park Commission power not only to issue bonds, but to "establish admission charges, build, restore, reconstruct any buildings, expend funds to hire or contract with historians, archaeologists, engineers and landscape planners, establish pay rates, and set up separate accounting records, and do virtually anything a private company could do to improve, maintain, or change its properties, without regard to regular state accounting or Civil Service procedures."

While the bill would provide for the historical restorations Williams wanted, there was a price which gave Williams pause: People had visited Fort Mackinac free for many years. Now they would have to pay. Even as some of his aides predicted severe public reaction, Governor Williams signed the bill. The historical development the bill made possible surpassed Williams' and Woodfill's wildest, fondest hopes.

WOODFILL COULD PLAN and prod, but he had a hotel to run and needed a professional to handle the kind of high-quality historical restoration he envisioned. Over the previous few years, the Park Commission had had offers of help from the Historical Commission's Dr. Lewis Beeson. Woodfill took up his offer.

Beeson turned for help to Dr. Eugene T. Petersen, director of the small State Museum in Lansing. Petersen had revitalized the museum's displays, but he had little more to do and only $300 a year to do it with. Young and energetic, Petersen was eager for a challenge. The commission established a new "Fort Mackinac Division" to handle the bond proceeds and named Petersen its director. The commission agreed to pay the Historical Commission $2,645 for

FAR LEFT: Dirk Gringhuis and Dr. Petersen discuss a mural for the Fort Mackinac Museum.

FAR LEFT: Dirk Gringhuis and Dr. Petersen discuss a mural for the Fort Mackinac Museum.

LEFT: Girl Scouts at the Avenue of Flags. Girls have served with distinction since 1974.

Petersen's services, but insisted it be clearly on record that the Park Commission, not the Historical Commission, was in charge of the project.

Woodfill and Petersen established immediate rapport. Woodfill had ideas and soon would have money. Petersen had expertise and enthusiasm. When Woodfill said in January he wanted the museum to open in June, Petersen didn't even blink. He looked forward to the opportunity to spend some real money on a worthwhile project. In meeting that deadline, he moved much faster than the commission. It was nearly May before the commission authorized $125,000 of 15-year bonds to pay for the job. The first $50,000 worth were not actually sold until June 7, a week before the museum would open.

Woodfill made it clear that Petersen was to work on the same model as Grand Hotel: contract outside for nearly everything. Petersen enlisted the support of Victor Hogg, an artist and curator at Michigan State University Museum, and Dirk Gringhuis, a commercial artist and book illustrator with a love for history. Hogg's creative genius produced the plan and Gringhuis, a master muralist, provided large and striking graphics.

Petersen and his contract crew assisted by Superintendent Nordberg's park employees worked frantically through the spring to prepare the fort for its reopening. Graffiti on the blockhouse walls was painted over and flagpoles were installed in an Avenue of Flags leading from the carriage stop to the new ticket booth. In the Soldiers' Barracks, which previously housed a display of old carriages, a chronological exhibit of Fort Mackinac's history was crafted from a few

historical objects and some large murals.

The project was doable only because Fort Mackinac already existed, with its 14 historic buildings—however dilapidated—and because the view from the ramparts was spectacular. The fort's brooding presence dominates the town, making it a landmark for all visitors as they arrive.

Woodfill was an avid memo writer. He liked to work through the night and did his own typing. By morning he had generated piles of memos, to be hand-delivered by personal messenger. Later in the morning Woodfill would call the recipients to see how things were going and be sure his instructions were followed.

Because it would be some time before the Commission's bonds were sold, Woodfill advanced his own cash to cover expenses. He expected to be repaid from admission fees at Fort Mackinac that first summer, but in a memo to Park Commissioner (and secretary) Henry E. Naegely, wrote that if the advances "for any reason can not be repaid . . . it is to be considered by me and by your Commission as a gift or donation."

Admission fees for the Fort were set at 50 cents for adults and 25 cents for children six to 10. Children under six got in free. Visitors bought metal

development in 1958. It had a recorded history of more than 300 years. It was on a major highway, I-75, and the new Mackinac Bridge was drawing great public attention. Mackinac had been a tourist attraction for more than 100 years, and now the tourist industry was growing fast. Few other locations in the nation were as well positioned. Now, in revenue bonds, the Park Commission had found a way to pay for development.

At the end of the 1958 season, Woodfill approached Petersen to see if he would stay on as permanent Director of Historic Projects. It didn't take Petersen long to say yes. It had been exhilarating to have money to develop a new museum in such a spectacular place, and the public's response had been beyond his imagination.

The commission was delighted as well, and at their September 15, 1958 meeting they authorized the sale of another $75,000 in bonds for improvements to Fort Mackinac. Governor Williams himself came to the December meeting to congratulate the members and tell them how pleased he was with their success.

The future of the Mackinac State Parks seemed assured, and the potential unlimited.

tokens, then inserted them in turnstiles at the fort gates. Woodfill insisted that there be no free admissions, and controls were tight. Woodfill himself paid every time he entered the Fort.

It had been tradition for a century for island visitors to visit the fort. Not even an admissions charge was new; it had been tried in the 1930s with some success. Still, no one knew how many would actually come. The $50,000 in bonds that financed the first year's work were sold at a bid to yield 5.5 percent—a bid based on projected revenue of $25,375 from 58,000 visitors. The projections turned out to be very conservative.

On June 15 the Fort Mackinac museum opened, on time, but with little ceremony. And the people came. And they loved it. The first summer, visitors deposited 118,000 tokens in the turnstiles, generating $54,119—enough to repay the entire debt and meet most of the operating expense.

Mackinac was uniquely situated for historical

11 Spanning the Straits

ABOVE:

The Mackinac Bridge under construction.

RIGHT: The bridge connects the night sky with light from Mackinaw City to St. Ignace.

SINCE THE 1880s, people had contemplated a bridge across the Straits of Mackinac. At first, rail cars were ferried across in boats equipped with tracks. Early automobiles were carried across on flatcars. In 1923, the state began car-ferry service, but that was iffy in winter and eventually just insufficient. Sometimes, as at the opening of deer season, motorists often spent whole days in line for the ferry.

The first Mackinac Bridge Authority, established in 1934, considered several plans, including a tunnel, or bridges that would hopscotch from Cheboygan to St. Ignace by way of Bois Blanc and Round islands. Some said the state had too much invested in ferries to build a bridge at all. Depression and war delayed the project for years.

A new Bridge Authority, established in 1950, quickly decided on a suspension bridge, approved $100 million in bonds, and broke ground in 1954—May 7 in St. Ignace and May 8 in Mackinaw City. The project required the largest marine-construction fleet ever assembled. In four summers crews poured nearly a million tons of concrete and tightened a million bolts. They drove almost 5 million rivets, wound 41,000 miles of steel wire into two 24-inch cables 8,600 feet long, and applied 160 tons of paint. The bridge opened November 1, 1957—just in time for deer season—and was formally dedicated the next June. About 1.4 million vehicles crossed the first year, half again as many as had ever crossed on ferries, and the yearly total still routinely sets records.

The bridge forever changed the Straits, especially Michilimackinac State Park. For one thing, the bridge approach ran right through the park, splitting it in half. Since construction would mean a lot of digging along the shore, the commission even discussed hiring an archaeologist to monitor the site and retrieve artifacts. Nothing was done at the time, but the discussions planted seeds for what blossomed into the nation's longest-running archaeological excavation.

As an important link in the interstate highway system that brought the Straits within a few hours of major population centers, it drew hundreds of thousands of new visitors to Mackinac and was a tourist attraction in itself. Many who crossed did so just to be crossing, but the original, $3.75 toll made many content simply to stay overnight in Mackinaw City and look at the bridge. New navigation lights on the bridge let the Old Mackinac Point Lighthouse and Fog Signal Station be deactivated and turned over to the Park Commission for use as a maritime museum. The Park Commission built a new Visitor's Center beneath the bridge approach, to serve both Michilimackinac west of the bridge and the new maritime museum being developed east of it. The maritime museum did not draw enough visitors to justify the expense and was closed in the late 1980s. The grounds became today's picnic area.

Perhaps as important as any of these effects of the bridge was the way it was financed—revenue bonds—provided a model for the Park Commission to follow when it decided a few years later to develop its historic resources.

12 # Broader Vision

A Chinese porcelain tea cup excavated at Michilimackinac demonstrates the richness of life at the Straits.

IN ITS FIRST SUMMER, 1958, the renovated Fort Mackinac generated so much money from admissions fees that Park Commission Chairman W. Stewart Woodfill likened it to an oil well. He and his new director of historic projects, Dr. Eugene T. Petersen, immediately began talking about whether they might find more "oil" with similar improvements on the mainland.

While the first of the Park Commission's revenue bonds went to improve Fort Mackinac, the program was intended from the start to include Michilimackinac in Mackinaw City and Fort DeBuade in St. Ignace. Peterson and Woodfill discussed both, but their focus quickly narrowed to Michilimackinac after a meeting in St. Ignace with supporters of rebuilding Fort DeBuade. The local enthusiasts insisted on having a major role in any development there, and the autocratic Woodfill was not about to let himself be hamstrung by citizen input. Besides, the exact site of the fort had never been found anyway.

At Michilimackinac, the exact site of the fort was known, thanks to an extensive survey in 1913. Better, the Park Commission owned the land. This seemed a much better place to look for more oil, and it was not long before they found one. Preliminary excavation at Michilimackinac revealed not only a fort, but a whole 18th-century village just below the sod, waiting to be revealed. The find was so exciting that by year's end, the commission had authorized another $500,000 in revenue bonds and sold $150,000 worth to get the project started. Meanwhile, Dr. Petersen brought in architects and museum

designers to plan the fort's reconstruction so the commission might have an income-generating museum by the summer of 1960. The archaeological excavations begun in 1959 have continued at Michilimackinac each summer since.

As soon as winter broke in 1960, crews began reconstructing the Soldiers' Barracks and the east half of the stockade walls. Turnstiles like the ones at Fort Mackinac were placed in a special opening in the East Palisade. Fort Michilimackinac opened on June 26, 1960.

However exciting it was as archaeology, Michilimackinac was hardly the quick financial success Fort Mackinac had been. The commission projected 225,000 visitors a year and $101,250 in revenue, but it took seven years to reach that attendance level. Only 151,774 passed through the turnstiles the first summer. While Colonial Michilimackinac did not quite gush revenue from the start, it had a wealth of artifacts and historical displays and quickly became self-supporting. This was partly because of cost controls. The Park Commission's entire Historic Projects Division had only two full time staff: Dr. Petersen and his wife, Marian, who handled the accounting and office functions. Everyone else was either seasonal or contractual. Additional staff were added only slowly as historical developments grew.

Historical research in the course of the Michilimackinac project uncovered a journal from the late 18th century, and when a copy was sent to Chairman Woodfill, he agreed with Dr. Petersen that it be published and offered for sale. Published in 1960, the *Doctor's Secret Journal* sold out. It

LEFT: The British red ensign waves over reconstructed Fort Michilimackinac.

BELOW: The commission and staff gathered for a meeting at the Fort Mackinac schoolhouse. Beginning at the right going counter clockwise around the table are W. Stewart Woodfill, Joseph H. Thompson, Eugene T. Petersen, Mariana B. Rudolph, Walter J. Murray, James P. Dunnigan, Carl A. Nordberg, Neil Downing, and W. F. Doyle. Marian Petersen is taking notes in back.

was the start of the Park Commission publications program that has included both popular and scholarly work, and which has won national recognition.

The expanded activity at Michilimackinac prompted expansion of the Park Commission as well, and in 1958 the legislature added a seventh member, designated a resident commissioner from Mackinaw City. The first one was Neil Downing, a Mackinaw City businessman.

Reconstruction of the fort meant dedicating the west half of the park to historical development, so the park's old Mackinaw City campground was moved east of the new bridge. The Old Mackinac Point Lighthouse there, abandoned when navigation lights were added to the new bridge, was turned over to the Park Commission for eventual use as a Maritime Museum.

As work progressed at Michilimackinac, exhibits were also being added or improved

RIGHT: Early excavations at
Michilimackinac.

The boardwalk
leading from the
west end of town.

through the early 1960s in a number of Fort Mackinac buildings on the island.

The Commission's efforts were recognized in 1961 when the National Park Service designated both Fort Michilimackinac and Mackinac Island as National Historic Landmarks, the highest honor that can be awarded. The award for Mackinac Island was based not only on the significance of the fort, but also on other commission projects, such as the Mission Church, Beaumont Memorial and the Biddle House.

Admission fees at the two forts were pumping considerable amounts of money into the commission's coffers, and it was tempting to use money generated by the historic programs for projects only loosely associated with the forts. Commissioner Woodfill saw two problems in particular that he thought the revenue-bond program might fix. One was the proliferation of garish business signs in the main business district on Mackinac Island, and the other was the crumbling wooden boardwalk along half a mile of lake front from the Iroquois hotel to the beach below the Grand.

He negotiated an arrangement with the City of Mackinac Island whereby the City Council would adopt a restrictive sign ordinance in exchange for the Park Commission's rebuilding the boardwalk. It was of small concern to Woodfill that the boardwalk was not in the State Park. Drawing on his experience with the old Park and Harbor Commission, he simply had the State Park acquire easements to the land under the boardwalk. In 1962 the walk was rebuilt at a cost of $30,000, and the city dutifully passed the sign ordinance, which is still in effect.

Woodfill's solutions seemed sound at first, but did not last long. The sign ordinance was only loosely enforced, when it was enforced at all, and the boardwalk soon rotted. Maintaining it caused chronic friction between the City of Mackinac Island and the Park Commission until 1985, when the state legislature appropriated money to rebuild it and give it to the city, if the city would keep it up. The next year, the boardwalk became the city's again.

Marquette Park also needed renovating in the 1960s, and again the revenue-bond fund was tapped for that, too. The old gravel sidewalks were removed, a sprinkler system was installed, and a wide variety of lilacs were planted in beds carefully planned by landscape architect Milton Baron. The grass now remains green all summer despite very heavy public use, and the open space is popular for sunbathing, lounging, picnicking and even occasional weddings and concerts.

DURING THE EARLY 1960s Michigan adopted a new state constitution which, among other things, consolidated more than 125 boards, commissions and agencies into no more than 20 departments. The hitherto independent Mackinac Island State Park Commission found a new home in the bureaucracy as part of the Department of Conservation—now the Department of Natural Resources. The Park Commission, however, had a special designation, called "Type I," that let it retain its statutory authority and operate as a semi-autonomous agency.

As a working relationship developed between

BELOW: The end of a yacht race fills the harbor and town.

the Commission and Conservation Department, the Park Commission's close connections with the governor proved important. In 1966 when the Park Commission and Conservation Commission met together for the first time, members of the Park Commission only half-jokingly promised not to take over the department. The comment was received with the same good humor with which it was offered, and over the years there has been little conflict and much cooperation between both staffs and commissions.

The two agencies had been cooperating for some time anyway in developing the yacht harbor on Mackinac. The Park Commission had developed the first small yacht dock there in the late 1920s, collecting small fees from boats docking there. Carl Nordberg, Park Superintendent from 1945 to 1967, had first come to the Island

RIGHT: Inside the Indian Dormitory, dedicated in 1966 as a museum.

The Carriage Tours' three horse hitch.

as a harbor manager in 1941. The expense of caring for the docks in the 1950s, however, outstripped the income they produced. When a more extensive harbor was needed, the Park Commission turned to the Michigan Waterways Commission.

From its small percentage of gasoline-tax revenues, the Waterways Commission had funds to build and operate harbors around the state. In 1959, at the Park Commission's request, the legislature transferred jurisdiction of the Mackinac Island harbor, between the Coast Guard Station and the Yoder Dock, south of Huron Street, to the Waterways Commission. The Waterways Commission designed and built new yacht dock facilities. Since then, the staffs of both agencies have cooperated closely.

While most get to Mackinac by water, the island has an airport as well. Built in 1934 and rebuilt in 1965, it is a vital link in winter. Before runway lights were added in the 1980s, emergency night flights required trucks to be lined up with their headlights on the runway. An air taxi regularly flies to and from St. Ignace, and islanders still talk about the time its engine failed on takeoff and pilot Paul Fullerton skillfully glided to a near-perfect landing on the narrow, rocky beach at British Landing. Flights now are routine, and Mackinac may be the only place on earth where the cab that takes you to the airport is drawn by a horse.

During the change in the structure of state government the Park Commission's internal structure underwent a significant adjustment as

well. From the beginning of the revenue-bond program, the director of historic projects, Dr. Eugene T. Petersen, and Park Superintendent Carl Nordberg, had functioned as equals. While they cooperated closely most of the time, tensions inevitably arose. Park Commission reports reveal that their respective authorities had "often been overlapping, duplicative, and at times confusing to the Commissioners and others."

In the summer of 1966, Dr. Petersen tendered his resignation, saying he was taking a job at the Henry Ford Museum in Dearborn, Michigan. He cited as one reason the divided responsibility for park leadership, calling it a "two-headed monster." Rectify that problem, he suggested, and he might stay.

The commission accepted his idea, refused his resignation, and agreed to name a single administrative head. On July 2, 1966, commissioners established the office of "director," to whom the superintendent would report. Dr. Petersen agreed to stay, was designated acting director immediately, and later was confirmed as director.

The timing of the reorganization was important because the commission was on the verge of issuing a new, $1 million bond issue which would provide funds for years of restoration, reconstruction and development. It was clear that the Park Commission had come to appreciate fully the importance of its historic assets.

13 Michilimackinac

FOR ALL THE HISTORY embodied in the Straits of Mackinac, none of the Mackinac Island State Park Commission's undertakings has brought more recognition and acclaim than the development of Colonial Michilimackinac.

This park, the most visible of the Mackinac State Historic Parks to the passerby on I-75, has

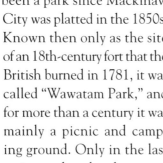
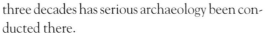

been a park since Mackinaw City was platted in the 1850s. Known then only as the site of an 18th-century fort that the British burned in 1781, it was called "Wawatam Park," and for more than a century it was mainly a picnic and camping ground. Only in the last three decades has serious archaeology been conducted there.

Michilimackinac State Park.

In 1904 the town gave the land to the state, and in 1909 the legislature renamed it "Michilimackinac State Park" and gave it to the Park Commission to manage. The Park Commission was not exactly overjoyed. The legislature had just halved the commission's appropriations and now was adding even more responsibility—and for land that was not even on Mackinac Island. To make matters worse, the legislature told the commission to spend five percent of the reduced appropriations on the new park. After a formal acceptance ceremony, the commission spent little money there until 1913.

That year, an increased appropriation from Lansing allowed the commission to buy 25 cement benches and a new flagpole for Michili-

mackinac, and to hire a groundskeeper named George W. Marshall for $5 a month. Of much greater significance, the new appropriation allowed the Park Commission to undertake the first-ever complete survey of all its lands, including Michilimackinac. One thing the survey revealed was solid evidence of the exact site of Fort Michilimackinac and some of the buildings there.

It was the start of something big, and there is reason to believe the commission sensed it. The commission offered Monsignor Frank A. O'Brien, president of the Michigan Historical Commission, permission to excavate the fort's 18th-century chapel. While nothing came of the offer, it demonstrated that the commission understood the archaeological potential of this park that, four years before, it had not even wanted.

Archaeological potential aside, the thing that made Michilimackinac into an important park was the automobile. Until 1915, the only development there beside those benches and that flagpole, had been a half-mile concrete walk along the shore. The automobile soon transformed Michilimackinac into a picnic and camping spot for thousands.

It was this popularity which, in the 1920s, prompted the Park Commission to develop the site of the old fort, hoping it would attract yet more visitors to the park. In 1930, new stockades erected at Fort Mackinac on the island were so impressive that the commission decided to reconstruct the old blockhouses and stockade at Michilimackinac, as well.

The commission bought 3,000 10-foot cedar

RIGHT: Fort and bridge from the northwest bastion.

BELOW: A redcoat sentry stands guard at the fort's Land Gate.

posts, and by the next spring had had points cut on 2,000 of them. But as the Depression deepened, money ran out and the poles simply lay on the ground until 1933. Even after Commissioner Roger Andrews decided something should be done with them, there was some uncertainty over what that would be. In the three years they had lain there, historical research had revealed that the original stockade's poles had been eight feet longer. Those being Depression days, the commission decided to use the poles on hand.

They would be placed, however, on the orig-

The 1933 stockade with the campground in the background.

inal location, as revealed by historic maps and confirmed by traces of palisade which Michilimackinac's manager, Chris Schneider, had found. The complete palisade was staked out, and then a serious problem was discovered: The northwest corner of the fort site was not on State Park land.

The commission had already added two blocks of land so the whole fort would be within the park, and now it realized it needed yet more. Making matters worse, the owner of the necessary land, Burrett Hamilton, was reluctant to sell. When the commission asked the Attorney General to initiate condemnation proceedings, however, Hamilton took the hint and decided to donate three lots to the Park Commission in exchange for the erection of a suitable bronze tablet recognizing the gift.

The decision was in the nick of time; reconstruction was so far along that plans were already being made for the fort's dedication. That cere-

mony, on July 1, 1933, included a speech by Governor William A. Comstock, and a reenactment of the Indians' 1763 attack on the fort. The reenactment tradition begun that day at Michilimackinac continues still.

For the next 20 years, through the Depression and World War II, little more was done at Fort Michilimackinac. Interest in the archaeological possibilities did not revive until the 1950s, but even then revival was slow. The first glimmer came when construction of the Mackinac Bridge was imminent and the commission considered asking a University of Michigan archaeologist to retrieve any artifacts unearthed by earthmovers. Nothing was done at the time, but the new interest in archaeology would soon grow into what has become the nation's oldest continuous archaeological dig.

The Park Commission dragged its feet even after Governor G. Mennen Williams summoned them to a high-level meeting in Detroit in November, 1955, to seek action on historic preservation. Two more years passed with little action. Finally, in 1957, Governor Williams had the dynamic owner of Grand Hotel, W. S. Woodfill, named chairman of the commission. Soon the commission had been authorized to sell bonds to finance such projects, and things began to move fast.

In the summer of 1959, the park's director of historical projects, Dr. Eugene T. Petersen, hired Dr. Moreau Maxwell, an archaeologist at Michigan State University, to do test excavations at Michilimackinac. Dr. Maxwell began his digging in an area referred to on ancient maps as the

"parade ground." He chose that area because he would be unlikely to find the remains of buildings there, and so could get a sense of the site's soil stratigraphy. Within a few days, however, the crew encountered a puzzling stone wall. Further historical research with the help of Dr. George May of the Michigan Historical Commission indicated that what they had found was the foundation of the Soldiers' Barracks built in 1769—after the maps were drawn.

The foundations clearly marked the site of the building, and the discovery of 18th-century artifacts confirmed its date. Michilimackinac had not been destroyed by relic collectors, as many thought. A whole 18th-century village lay just below the sod, waiting to be revealed by professional archaeologists and reconstructed by skilled historians, architects and craftsmen. Thus began a series of archaeological excavations which have been conducted at Michilimackinac each summer since 1959.

Dr. Maxwell formally reported his exciting findings to the Park Commission that December, and at the same meeting the commission authorized bonds to finance the reconstruction.

As financing was still being finalized, Dr. Petersen and his team of architects and museum designers were already at work so Michilimackinac would be open and producing revenue the next summer. Richard Frank, a young Lansing architect interested in historic architecture, was hired to draw plans for an authentic reconstructions of the palisade and the 1769 Soldiers' Barracks. The latter, 88 by 22 feet, would house an interpretive museum already being designed and fabricated by the same team that had designed the new museum at Fort Mackinac: Victor Hogg, artist and curator at Michigan State University Museum, and artist-illustrator Dirk Gringhuis.

As soon as winter broke in 1960, work began. The campground was moved east of the Mackinac Bridge and the west half of the park was dedicated to historical development. Crews began reconstructing the Soldiers' Barracks and the east half of the stockade walls. Turnstiles were placed in a special opening in the east palisade. At the other end of the park, east of the bridge, the abandoned Old Mackinac Point Lighthouse was turned over to the Park Commission for use as an eventual maritime museum. Fort Michilimackinac opened on June 26, 1960. That summer's paid admissions of 151,774, while not the 250,000 projected, were certainly respectable for a fort that was only partly reconstructed.

Reconstruction continued through the 1960s, a few buildings each year as research time and money permitted. The second year, 1961, the palisade and blockhouses were completed and the King's Storehouse reconstructed. In 1962, the English Traders' Rowhouse was added, with

BELOW: Canoe brigade approaching Michilimackinac.

OPPOSITE RIGHT: Open-fire cooking evokes the smells of the past.

OPPOSITE FAR RIGHT: Flintlock muskets resound on the parade ground.

its unique archaeological tunnel, as were three French Trader Houses outside the fort walls. The Commanding Officer's House followed in 1963, and the Church of Ste. Anne was reconstructed in 1964.

The commission's work won high recognition in 1961 when the National Park Service designated both Fort Michilimackinac and Mackinac Island as National Historic Landmarks—the highest honor that can be awarded.

In the course of his historical research early in the project, the Historical Commission's Dr. May found a journal written in 1768-1772 by Dr. Daniel Morison and containing many details about life at Michilimackinac. Moreover, its details of the scandalous behavior of an Ensign Robert Johnstone made it fascinating reading as well as good history. Park Commission Chairman Woodfill, who loved books, agreed with Dr. Petersen that the commission should publish it. *The Doctor's Secret Journal*, edited by Dr. May, and illustrated by Dirk Gringhuis, went on sale in the spring of 1960 and quickly sold out. It was the first in an ongoing Park Commission publishing program of both popular and scholarly titles.

BY THE MID-1960s the Park Commission realized it was onto something big at Michilimackinac, and hired the Ann Arbor planning firm of Johnson, Johnson and Roy to do a broad master plan.

Among the plan's important features were exclusion of automobiles from the historic area west of the Mackinac Bridge, and planting of a visual barrier between the historic area and the modern world beyond. Within the fort, the plan called for continued reconstruction of buildings as located by archaeology. Elsewhere, the firm recommended eliminating the camping area (and working with the DNR to provide camping elsewhere) and development of a maritime park in the area east of the bridge, including the lighthouse. The plan also envisioned a new park welcome center under the Mackinac Bridge approach that would serve as an entrance for both the historic fort area west of the bridge and the new maritime park east of it.

The plan provided general direction, and the million-dollar bond issue envisioned by the Park Commission assured years of continuing reconstruction.

To carry out the ambitious plans, the Park Commission expanded the staff in 1967. The first step was to hire a new assistant director, Dr. David A. Armour, who had been an assistant professor of history at the University of Wisconsin-Milwaukee. He knew Michilimackinac well, having worked in the archaeology program during the summers of 1965 and 1966, and having supervised the interpretation staff both there and on the island.

The next step lay in bolstering the archaeological effort. From 1959 to 1969 the Park Commission had contracted with Michigan State University to conduct archaeological excavations at Michilimackinac, and with the University of Michigan for exploring the fort well and a military dump on Mackinac Island. Academic archaeologists had time to dig in the summer, but the

BELOW: Each Memorial Day the residents of Mackinaw City reenact the stirring events of 1763.

BELOW: Each Memorial Day the residents of Mackinaw City reenact the stirring events of 1763.

ings from Michilimackinac available to scholars around the world. Dr. Stone had previously co-authored a book with J. Jefferson Miller of the Smithsonian Institution, titled *Ceramics of Michilimackinac*. Archaeology at Michilimackinac had come of age, and these books brought international repute to the program.

Subsequent archaeological reports have been published by Dr. Donald P. Heldman, who replaced Stone as staff archaeologist in 1975. Much of the research generated by Mackinac Island State Park Commission programs has been reported in two publications, *Reports in Michigan History* and *Archaeology and Archaeological Completion Report Series*.

rest of the year, when reports on the excavations needed to be written, they had teaching obligations. Although MSU's Dr. Maxwell and Lewis Binford published their 1959 findings, reports often did not keep up with reconstruction plans. Excavation had also produced a backlog of thousands of artifacts to be processed and analyzed. The Park Commission, realizing that the Michilimackinac Archaeology Project was too big for mere seasonal involvement, hired its first full-time, staff archaeologist.

The staff archaeologist was Lyle Stone, a Ph.D candidate whose dissertation research focused on the Michilimackinac excavations. He eventually received his Ph.D, and his dissertation, somewhat revised, was jointly published by the Park Commission and the Michigan State University Museum. Titled *Fort Michilimackinac 1715-1781*, it was heavily illustrated and made find-

ALTHOUGH MOST EXCAVATION at Michilimackinac has been inside the palisade, two summers went into excavation near the new parking lot between the bridge and the fort, known in the 18th century as the "subarbs." Remains of several 18th-century houses were located there, and other possible house sites were identified by electronic surveys.

After 35 years of continuous excavation, approximately half of the fort interior has been explored. Several areas, designated as archaeological preserves, will not be excavated. Still, many valuable and exciting discoveries await the archaeologist's trowel at Michilimackinac.

Reconstruction within the fort has been concentrated in the northwest and southeast quadrants. Work has hewed to a philosophy of restoring buildings so they look as much as possible as they did in the 1770s, but with materials that will

THE *WELCOME*

When the Park Commission operated its Maritime Museum at the Old Mackinac Point Lighthouse, one of the central exhibits was the sloop *Welcome*. This was a replica of a 55-footer built at Michilimackinac in 1775 by the wealthy trader John Askin and operated on lakes Michigan, Huron and Erie. Her original log survives and tells of many trips between Michilimackinac and Mackinac Island in 1780, when the British moved there during the American Revolution. In 1971, the commission decided to build a replica of the *Welcome* to celebrate the U. S. Bicentennial in 1976. Naval architect Frederick S. Ford Jr. based his plans on drawings of a similar vessel from archives in Greenwich, England, and Ted McCutcheon Sr. of Charlevoix took charge of construction. The keel was laid in 1972, and work went on in the park under a plastic-covered shelter. More than 1 million visitors watched *Welcome* being built. Her final cost, however, was more than double early estimates of $200,000, and she wasn't launched until 1980, four years after the Bicentennial. When she finally was hoisted into the water at the Mackinaw City

Marina, she seemed far smaller than she had on dry land. On her maiden voyage in July, 1981, she was greeted by an enthusiastic crowd at Mackinac Island during the island's centennial. But when she went back on display in Mackinaw City, visitors were content simply to look at her from the dock. Not enough paid to go aboard to cover maintenance costs. By 1989 she had begun to rot, and she was leased to the Maritime Heritage Alliance in Traverse City for restoration and use in educational projects.

THE MICHILIMACKINAC STORY

RIGHT: Sunset over Lake Michigan.

OPPOSITE RIGHT: Michilimackinac visitors await the cannon's roar.

last longer. All wood in contact with the ground is pressure-treated with copper sulfates, and most of the buildings have modern concrete footings.

A unique feature of the museum at Michilimackinac is its underground galleries. One clearly tells the story of archaeology at Michilimackinac and preserves some of the original ruins, including a French well and a storage cellar. The other gallery, providing an entrance to the reconstructed Powder Magazine, was made possible in part by the nature of the British effort to destroy it. In 1781, after building a new fort on Mackinac Island, the British deliberately burned the original magazine building at Michilimackinac. Its dirt roof collapsed, however, smothering the fire and preserving the charred floorboards and log walls. Carefully excavated and preserved, these remains can be viewed from the subterranean gallery. These underground exhibits literally give Michilimackinac far more museum galleries than appear on the surface.

Interpretation of history at Michilimackinac is offered in several forms. Originally all the displays were behind glass, which allowed a limited staff to operate the fort. Now, with a larger staff, many glass barriers have been removed, and interpreters in 18th-century costume bring the fort to life. Venison stew simmers over the coals in a fireplace, providing tasty meals for the interpretive staff. Booming musket and cannon draw crowds. The church is the scene of regular reenactments of a French wedding, after which the audience is invited to participate in a lively wedding dance. Another dramatic reenactment portrays the arrival of voyageurs and traders at the post to conduct the fur trade upon which 18th-century Michilimackinac depended.

The living-history program has been expanded in recent years to include Indians, who were historically by far the majority population in the area. Though the story of native peoples was long presented in park museums, Ottawa and Chippewa still living in the Straits area were antagonized by early portrayals of the Indians' 1763 capture of the fort. Lurid displays emphasized the bloody events of the battle, and the annual reenactment by the citizens of Mackinaw City was billed as "The Massacre." During the late 1960s, after local Indians protested, the reenactment was renamed "The Pageant." It continues to be improved through scholarship and training, and exhibits and displays have been modified to reflect the victorious Indian attack. The Indians' role in today's living-history program is based on extensive historical research and conversations with local Native American leaders. Many of the interpretive staff are of Native American descent. The setting outside the fort stockade now represents a camp of Indians who have come to Michilimackinac to trade. The response, both by the public and the local Indian people, has been very positive.

The welcome center envisioned in that master plan 30 years ago was completed in 1971, with large glass windows overlooking the Straits, an audiovisual-program theater and a museum shop. Nowadays, it welcomes three times as many visitors in a busy month as Michilimackinac had in a whole year back in the 1920s, when the fort was first being reconstructed.

14 Mill Creek

IN 1972, AN AMATEUR HISTORIAN and archaeologist from Cheboygan named Ellis Olson was prospecting with his metal detector for the site of a gristmill on Mill Creek, which flows into the Straits of Mackinac about three miles east of Mackinaw City.

He had found a log from the original mill dam still in the creek bed, and nearby he unearthed what appeared to be a brass badge or insignia plate. Olson brought the find to Dr. Lyle Stone, the Mackinac Island State Park Commission's staff archaeologist, who showed it, in turn, to Dr. David Armour, an historian and assistant director of the parks. As they discussed and examined the brass artifact, they realized that it was the brass insignia plate from a cap worn by one of the British soldiers who had captured Fort Mackinac in 1812.

The Mill Creek site begged for further exploration, even though it was not on State Park land. After getting the DNR's permission, Dr. Stone spent a few days checking the heavily wooded site, trowel in hand. He found a depression in the ground with a small mound nearby, which suggested a cellar and chimney, and began to dig. The artifacts he found, including military buttons, dated the site to the late 18th century and early 19th century.

A check of historical documents revealed that the land, known as Private Claim 334, had been the site of a sawmill and, later, a gristmill. Owned first by Robert Campbell, it had later been sold to a prominent Mackinac Island merchant named Michael Dousman. This Mackinac Island connection led Stone and the Park Commission to continue excavations there, even if not quite on the scale of the ongoing dig at Michilimackinac.

A crew led by a graduate student, Patrick Martin, worked there in 1973, 1974 and 1975, and located the sites of the mill dam, a barn and two houses—one on each side of the creek. It was clear that a substantial community had existed at Mill Creek from the 1780s until the 1840s, and that it had close ties with Fort Mackinac and Mackinac Island.

In 1975, on the basis of this evidence, the Mackinac Island State Park Commission persuaded the Michigan Legislature to transfer the 500-acre tract from the Forestry Division to the Park Commission. The commission got a grant in 1977 from the National Endowment for the Humanities to assess the site and develop a feasibility study and master plan for developing it.

Victor Hogg of River Bend Studios, who had been involved in museum development at both Fort Mackinac and Michilimackinac, undertook the study. He came up with an exciting concept that would blend historic reconstruction with the interpretation of the area's natural resources, to tell how people have used the land and its resources from the Ice Age to the present.

Calculating the costs of construction and operation, the commission projected that the Mill Creek park would draw enough visitors to meet operating costs out of admission fees. There would not be enough, however, to repay money borrowed for construction. The Park Commission approved the master plan, but directed staff to seek grants for the development.

Grants for the project, totalling more than

The brass British insignia plate that triggered the reconstruction at Historic Mill Creek

LEFT: Samuel A. Milstein of the DNR presents the Mill Creek deed to chairman Sheldon B. Smith. David A. Armour holds the drawing of the park's location.

BELOW: Before the sawmill was built all boards had to be sawn by hand.

LEFT: Beavers dam Mill Creek in several places creating placid pools.

BELOW LEFT AND RIGHT: The falling waters on the small Mill Creek provide power to drive the mill.

$200,000, came eventually from Coastal Zone Management of the U.S. Department of Commerce, the Upper Great Lakes Regional Commission, and the Land and Water Conservation Fund. The money made possible additional archaeology, construction of nature trails, and the reconstruction of the mill dam. It all took time, and construction had to be carefully planned so that each phase could remain dormant, perhaps for years, while additional funding was sought for the balance of the project.

In 1982, having spent the money from its million-dollar, 1966 revenue-bond issue, the Park Commission issued bonds to raise another $500,000, most of it earmarked for developing Old Mill Creek State Historic Park. (This was not as easy as it sounds. Soaring interest rates had gone beyond the limit set by the legislature when it authorized the commission to issue bonds in 1958. For the new bonds, the commission had to lobby for an amendment to that 1958 act, raising the interest-rate ceiling.)

For a time, the commission considered building a steam-powered railroad between Mill Creek and Mackinaw City. The idea was dropped after feasibility studies demonstrated that it would never generate enough revenue to recoup costs.

With fresh capital available, the Mill Creek project went on a fast track for a June 15, 1984, opening. Crews designed and erected an operating, water-powered sawmill. A Visitor's Center was built, comprising a museum and theater area and a restroom-concession building. Victor Hogg fabricated the museum exhibits and a new Park Commission staffer, Jeffery Dykehouse,

oversaw development and installation of a nine-projector audiovisual program.

From the day it opened Historic Mill Creek has proved very popular. The first year, 74,548 visitors explored the park—nearly twice the number projected in the feasibility study.

The park has been improved each year since it opened, and supplemental legislative appropriations have let the Park Commission keep Historic Mill Creek open in spring and fall, when there are not enough visitors to meet all operating expenses. The commission has won additional grants to develop and interpret nature trails, and build a wheelchair ramp up the bluff and a maple-sugar shack. Funds provided by the volunteer Mackinac Associates organization have helped pay for a summer naturalist who works with school children who come by the busload. The commission has bought additional land that once was part of Private Claim 334, and today's Historic Mill Creek park encompasses 625 acres.

Historic Mill Creek is evidence of the tremendous potential for park development based on historical aspects of the Straits of Mackinac. Historians and archaeologists are aware of many undeveloped historic sites on Round Island, Bois Blanc Island, the Upper Peninsula mainland, and in the Lower Peninsula outside of Mackinaw City. Given funds for developing such sites, and a reasonable hope of their being self-supporting, the Park Commission and staff welcome new challenges.

BELOW: The Straits of Mackinac with Fort Michilimackinac in the foreground.

sion depends on legislative appropriation.

The success of the museum programs at Fort Mackinac, Michilimackinac and Mill Creek have provided stable income and allowed steady expansion of the projects and of park staff relating to historical development. Legislative appropriations, however, have not been as stable. During the state's fiscal crisis in the 1980s, appropriations were drastically cut. While historical developments expanded, park operations were

static or even declined. That is where grants have helped.

The development of the area around British Landing is a glowing example. In 1976, through the efforts of Commissioner James P. Dunnigan, the Highway Department provided $70,000 to construct a rest area at British Landing. The new building replaced two primitive pit toilets which had become utterly inadequate for the hundreds of thousands of visitors to the island. The building was designed with a spacious lobby in hopes it could one day become a nature center. Now, after many years, the plan is reality, and that lobby houses a natural-history interpretation program run by a naturalist every day in summer. When annual traffic at British Landing rose to 400,000 bicyclists, walkers, drive-yourself carriages, and roller bladers, funds from the Coastal Zone Management program allowed a redesign of the entire area, including a nature trail and displays.

The Coastal Zone Management program, through a number of modest grants totaling $96,000, has had significant impact on the way people use the island park. One effort led to publication of a new map of island roads and trails. Another paid for planning of interpretive signs and landscaping along M-185, the shore road circling the island. Subsequent grants provided for the construction of a stone retaining wall and wooden safety fence below Arch Rock, for landscaping at British Landing, and for the construction of a wildflower trail. Other displays around the park enlighten visitors on such matters as wildlife, glaciers, fossils, trees, and erosion.

The Coastal Zone Management grants focus energy on significant park improvement projects, because the grants have to be matched 50-50 by park funds, and the park usually contributes its share in the form of staff time.

The Michigan Department of Transportation provided funds in the late 1980s to blacktop some interior park roads so bicyclists might use them. Land and Water Conservation funds helped pay for two hard-surface tennis courts. In the mid-1980s, unemployed young people in public-assistance programs cleared brush and fallen trees in the park. They also helped rebuild park trails and stairways, such as those to Fort Holmes and Point Lookout.

In 1994, a $25,000 grant paid for planting trees at the site of the former powerhouse on the east side of the island, at the service yard at British Landing, and along the east side of British Landing Road to screen the resource-recovery building.

Of perhaps the greatest impact on the island was the multi-million dollar replacement of water and sewer lines in 1983 and 1984, paid for by a combination of federal and state funds. Several miles of water and sewer lines were replaced, and a new water treatment plant built on the beach below Robinson's Folly. A new million-gallon reservoir replaced the old brick reservoir near Fort Holmes, and a smaller reservoir was built behind the Fort Mackinac service buildings. The new sewers led to a wastewater treatment plant built on State Park land in 1972 with a $258,000 state subsidy. They replaced sewers that emptied into the lake west of the Iroquois Hotel.

RIGHT: Sunlight glistens off Lake Huron at the Straits.

FAR RIGHT: Dennis Bradley shapes glowing iron in the Benjamin Blacksmith Shop.

As in earlier times, the State Park and the City of Mackinac Island often found their programs intertwined. When the state ceased using the old gravel pit between Harrisonville and the cemeteries, the area became a dump for stumps and forest debris. But Park Manager Rollie McCready envisioned the site as a recreation area for island people, and had it leveled off. Over the years park personnel and local volunteers leveled the site, and in 1984 the park granted a 20-year lease on it to the City of Mackinac Island to develop a recreation area. Now called Great Turtle Park, and managed for the city by Mackinac Island Recreation and Development group, it has a lighted ball diamond, children's play area, pavilion, riding ring, and basketball and volley ball court. Many of the facilities have been developed with State Park help.

DURING THE 19 YEARS that Dr. Petersen ran either the historical projects or the parks themselves as chief administrator, the Mackinac Island State Park Commission won recognition as one of the nation's premier historical agencies. It began in 1961 with designation as a National Historic Landmark. Many of the parks' historic structures, including Fort Mackinac itself, have been placed on the National Register of Historic Places. The Michigan Historical Commission has adorned many State Park buildings and places with historic markers.

In 1972, the Mackinac Island State Park Commission applied for accreditation by the American Association of Museums, which has a rigorous system for evaluating how well museums meet professional standards. A committee was assigned to evaluate the parks, and they scheduled a visit to Mackinac on September 4-7, 1973. In preparation, park staff completed pages and pages of questionnaires. Later in the year the effort was rewarded with formal accreditation, making Mackinac one of the first Michigan institutions so honored. The parks were re-accredited following a second visit in July, 1985.

An era came to an end in the spring of 1985, when Dr. Petersen retired as superintendent. When he retired, so did his wife, Marian, who had served efficiently as the Park Commission's office manager, chief fiscal officer, and administrative assistant.

Dr. Petersen had directed the Park Commission's programs for 27 years—19 of them as superintendent. A fiscal conservative, he had run a tight ship to keep expenses down, but he had trusted his staff and given them considerable operational freedom. By no means a bureaucrat, Dr. Petersen kept paperwork to a minimum and avoided formal meetings, preferring to conduct staff business over a cup of coffee. Many of his decisions as superintendent emerged from brainstorming sessions at the Fort Mackinac Tea Room, and numerous projects began as sketches on the backs of coffee-shop napkins.

Today's exciting living-history programs at Mackinac State Historic Parks, and the parks' reputation for archaeology and historical scholarship, are living testimony to his vision.

16 Fort Mackinac

Civil War re-enactors camp between Fort Mackinac and the Scout Barracks.

FROM ITS VERY INCEPTION, in 1895, the Mackinac Island State Park Commission recognized its responsibility to care for the historic buildings of Fort Mackinac. Today's authentically restored fort, however, did not come about until the 1950s, when the commission undertook a long-term commitment to developing historic assets. How Fort Mackinac came to be as it is today, with all the popular exhibits and living history, is a long and interesting story.

In the earliest years, most of the effort went to keep the buildings weather tight and painted. Whatever renovations the commission undertook were done to make buildings usable—often so they could be rented out to produce income. Redundant buildings were demolished to reduce maintenance expenses.

It was not until 1916 that the commission began using even portions of the fort as a museum. That came about when one of the commissioners, Judge Edwin O. Wood, donated his collection of firearms and Indian and pioneer relics. To house them, the Park Commission renovated the Officers' Stone Quarters in the fort, and Commissioner Walter O. Briggs donated three large, glass display cases. The Fort Museum, as it was called, was dedicated in 1922. The Park Commission developed a cooperative arrangement with the Michigan Historical Commission, of which Judge Wood was also a member, for expanding the Fort Museum. The collection there was augmented in the 1920s with relics from World War I, such as captured German machine guns. When a tea-room concession was estab-

lished on the lower floor of the Stone Quarters, the concessionaire was given the responsibility of maintaining the museum located on the main floor above.

In 1928, when G. A. Hendricks became chairman, he also became a driving force behind a revival of interest in the historical aspects of the commission program. Hendricks, head of a Grand Rapids furniture company, appreciated the importance of history on the island. He immediately urged the creation of a display of antique carriages and other horse-drawn equipment at the fort, in the main room of the Soldiers' Barracks. It would, he felt, be of particular interest on an island where no automobiles were allowed.

In 1929, Hendricks proposed a celebration in 1934 of the 300th anniversary of the discovery of the Straits by French explorer Jean Nicolet. In a letter to his fellow commissioners and Governor Fred W. Green, in April, 1929, Chairman Hendricks laid out his plans for historical preservation and development of Fort Mackinac, including reconstruction of the fort stockade.

Hendricks found an ally in Commissioner Roger M. Andrews, who knew how historic sites appeal to tourists. They secured $660 to buy 1,200 hewn, eight-foot cedar ties for stockade posts. For another $447, they obtained five-prong iron spikes from Jackson Prison, to put atop the stockade pickets. The new stockade, spikes and all, was erected in 1930. The iron spikes vanished over the years, removed one at a time by souvenir hunters, but most of the 1,200 cedar pickets remain. Their survival, untreated for 65 years in Mackinac weather, is evidence of the rot-resis-

tance of cedar—and of the foresight of the men who used it.

During the Depression, the National Park Service provided the Park Commission with the services of an architect, Warren L. Rindge, to compile a detailed historical and architectural report on the fort. Illustrated with his painstakingly measured drawings, it showed all the buildings more than 100 years old. Although somewhat tediously titled, Rindge's "Report on Existing Ramparts and Buildings at Old Fort Mackinac, on Mackinac Island, together with Recommendations for their Eventual Restoration" remains an invaluable record of the condition of the fort buildings in the mid-1930s.

Depression-era Civilian Conservation Corps

FORT MACKINAC

RIGHT: The East Blockhouse in 1967 was the first fort building to be completely restored.

BELOW: David Armour and Lyle Stone examine early foundations under the Quartermaster's Storehouse.

workers made extensive repairs to historic buildings at Fort Mackinac, replacing rotted sills, rebuilding the Soldiers' Barracks porch, and repairing crumbling stone walls. They installed steam pipes to heat buildings and created apartments in the Soldiers' Barracks.

Then along came World War II, and wartime rationing and travel curtailment drastically reduced summer crowds on Mackinac. Among the wartime casualties on the island were the fort's cannons—removed in 1942 during a scrap-metal drive. Later, when staff were questioned about the removal of the cannons, no one would take responsibility for removing them. Today, only two authentic, antique cannon barrels remain in the fort. One, in the Commissary theater, was donated shortly after the war by Commissioner Edward A. Ward. The other, a bronze barrel that fired a 12-pound ball, was purchased in the 1980s so there would be at least one authentic cannon of the type which had once guarded the fort. All the remainder of the cannons on public display are replicas.

In the mid-1950s Commissioner Margaret Price began urging her colleagues to attend more actively to the State Park's historic properties, and in November, 1955, Governor G. Mennen Williams began to prod the Park Commission into action. It was not easy, and that year he managed only to engender discussion about considering the advisability of creating a new Park and Harbor Authority that could issue bonds to pay for rehabilitating some buildings.

Pressure on the commission increased in 1956 when the Michigan State Medical Society complained openly about the commission's lack of care for the Beaumont Memorial, which had recently been renovated by private benefactors. Things finally began to move the next year when Governor Williams personally arranged to have the energetic, like-minded owner of Grand Hotel, W. S. Woodfill, named commission chairman.

Woodfill envisioned high-quality historical restoration, and knew he needed expert help. Early in 1958, he persuaded the Michigan Historical Commission to let the director of its State Museum in Lansing, Dr. Eugene T. Petersen, help out on Mackinac. Petersen, young and energetic, was eager for a new challenge, and Woodfill gave him one when he said he wanted a museum open

in Fort Mackinac by June.

Petersen got to work, and things moved so fast that sometimes the cart got before the horse. The commission's first formal interview with Dr. Petersen was on February 24, and not until April 28 did the commission agreed to pay the Historical Commission $2,645 for his services. By then, Petersen had already been approached about the possibility of becoming the commission's museum director at Fort Mackinac.

Petersen brought in a designer and artist, and to supplement the new museum's small initial collection of artifacts they used large and striking graphics to depict the history of the fort.

The team worked frantically with Park Superintendent Carl Nordberg's park crew to make the museum ready. Graffiti on the blockhouse walls was painted over, and flagpoles were installed in an Avenue of Flags leading from the carriage stop to the Fort. Since the whole project would be paid for by admissions revenue, a booth was erected where visitors would buy tokens to enter.

Petersen and Nordberg's crews installed the exhibits in the Soldiers' Barracks, which had previously housed that display of old carriages. Outside, the rest of the fort's 14 historic buildings—however dilapidated—served as exhibits unto themselves.

The museum was ready by Woodfill's deadline. The first year saw 118,000 tokens deposited in the turnstiles, enough to repay the bonds sold to finance the project as well as most of the operating expenses. Woodfill likened it to "an oil well which can pump funds into historical development at Mackinac indefinitely." After

that first year, Petersen was hired away from the Historical Commission to become the Park Commission's director of historic projects. He would go on to become park superintendent, and would remain until he retired in 1985.

FROM THAT START, the Park Commission went on in the 1960s to undertake major restoration at Fort Mackinac. The park's construction and restoration were handled internally, with crews working initially under the supervision of Frank and Stein, architects. Except for mechanical work—structural steel, electrical and plumbing systems—most tasks were done by park employees. The park's grounds crew foreman, "Rollie" McCready, served, in effect, as general contractor. Efforts were made to train the core crew in some trades by having them work alongside outside contractors.

Eventually the park workers became highly skilled in analyzing the way historic buildings had been built. They also became adept at masonry, carpentry, plastering, and other building trades. McCready was not afraid of any project, and the whole crew learned something with every new project. Many of the contract workmen, brought in for the job with a promise of five years' work, eventually became permanent park employees.

With work going on year-round, commissioners feared at first that visitors to the fort would object. Instead, the public enjoyed watching the restoration work, and were pleased to see what their admission fees were paying for.

Usually one building was tackled at a time and

Fort Mackinac

RIGHT: The barred door of the Fort Mackinac Guardhouse.

FAR RIGHT: Fort Mackinac's East Blockhouse in Autumn sunlight evokes a bygone era.

the methodical restoration of the buildings provided the master plan for museum development. The first building restored in Fort Mackinac was the East Blockhouse, in the summer of 1967. Next came the rear wall of the Soldiers' Barracks, which was severely rotted. Restoration often involved the removal of the apartments built in fort buildings during the 1930s. Carpenters frequently had to replace the sill logs, floor joists and flooring, which were usually seriously rotted.

The restorers' philosophy was to do as little as necessary to the original buildings, to preserve original building materials, to remove anything added after 1895, and to base the appearance of the buildings on the park's historic photographs.

As buildings were restored, interpretive exhibits were installed in them. The displays—usually period settings—reflected a variety of time periods in the fort's history, and exhibits were put behind glass to protect them.

As additional buildings were restored, the museum was relocated from the Soldiers' Barracks to the Commissary, and then returned to the Soldiers' Barracks. Eventually, it was dismantled and replaced by an audiovisual program in the Commissary.

The current philosophy governing Fort Mackinac is to focus on the period of the 1880s, when the fort looked much as it does today. As a result of funds from the National Endowment for the Humanities for a master planning study, a new interpretive museum is being planned for the second story of the Soldiers' Barracks.

Today's living-history exhibits at Fort Mackinac developed over the years. Originally, the fort's lone guide wore a red British uniform from the 1780s, when Fort Mackinac was constructed. Later, as interpretation focused on the dramatic events of the War of 1812, the guides wore uniforms of that period.

Then guided tours were developed, and the guides experimented with firing muskets and a small salute cannon. At first, many feared this would frighten horses and perhaps cause a runaway. But light charges held the reports down, and the island's horses became used to the noise. The public, of course, loved the action, and the firing of muskets and cannon became a significant part of the interpretive program.

The program began to expand in exciting new ways in 1982, when Phil Porter became curator of interpretation. Porter, who had a master's degree from the History Museum Studies Program at Cooperstown, New York, had been a Fort Mackinac Guide. He added military music to enliven the fort, and changed the guides' uniforms to those of "Wayne's Legion," from the days when American soldiers first occupied Fort Mackinac in 1796.

He instituted some dramatic reenactments, including a military court martial, and added women interpreters in the fort to create a domestic presence. New exhibits were installed with children in mind, such as the very popular Childrens' Discovery Room.

Today's interpretation of history at Fort Mackinac, more dynamic than ever, is being refined and augmented each year to keep the fort interesting for visitors.

17 Beyond Fort Walls

FOR ALL ITS EMPHASIS on restoring the old forts on Mackinac Island and at Michilimackinac, the Mackinac Island State Park Commission has undertaken many restorations outside fort walls. This is especially so on Mackinac Island. One of them, of course, is the turn-of-the-century cottage that is now the Governor's Summer Residence. Most of the restored buildings are far older than that.

Much of this work on the island had its beginnings in the 1930s, in the studies done by Warren L. Rindge, a Grand Rapids architect hired by the National Park Service. He surveyed all the Fort Mackinac buildings then more than a century old, and made extensive drawings of them. And in his work, he included three other historic buildings: the Mission Church, Biddle House, and Stuart House.

Mission Church

The Stuart House was restored in the 1940s by the Mackinac Island Park and Harbor Commission, and Depression work-relief crews did extensive work on fort buildings. But work on other buildings had to await the end of both the Depression and the war that followed. Even then, restoration was financed privately at first. Only after considerable prodding—and then somewhat reluctantly—did the Park Commission take on such projects.

One of the first downtown restorations was the old Earley House, which the Park Commis-

sion received as a gift in 1943 from the Parke, Davis Company, a pharmaceutical firm. It was significant to medical historians as the site of the 1822 shooting of Alexis St. Martin, on whom Dr. William Beaumont performed experiments. In making the gift, the company also pledged $5,000 to help restore the building, which became the Beaumont Memorial.

During World War II, the commission also accepted the offer of Frank D. McKay to buy the Biddle House, the oldest surviving residence on Mackinac Island, and give it to the park along with funds to help restore it.

Although it would be years before the Beaumont Memorial and Biddle House were restored and open to the public, the gifts helped focus the Park Commission's attention on such historic properties. One reason restoring them took so long was that during the war, private funds were scarce and state funds all but nonexistent.

Fortunately, however, two prominent architects were interested in the properties. One was Warren Rindge, who had scrutinized the Stuart and Biddle houses. The other was Professor Emil Lorch of the University of Michigan, whose interest lay in the Beaumont Memorial.

After the war, funds again became available for restoration efforts, but the Park Commission was not swift to move, preferring for a time to leave such projects to others who were more inclined.

In the early 1950s, two of these old buildings were leased to organizations that would take charge of restoration—the Beaumont Memorial to the Michigan Medical Society, and the Bid-

dle House to the Michigan Society of Architects. Spurred on by Adrian "Gus" Langius, the Michigan Builders Association also provided funds for restoring Biddle House. Once restored, both buildings were turned back over to the Park Commission to maintain.

By the 1960s, spurred on by Governor G. Mennen Williams, who had keen interest in both Mackinac and history, the Park Commission began doing restoration work in earnest.

One major project, dedicated in 1966 as a museum, was the Indian Dormitory. It had been built in 1838 by Indian Agent Henry Schoolcraft, on flat land beside the fort garden. He built it because the 1836 Treaty of Washington required a place for visiting Indians to stay while they conducted business with the Indian Agent.

It served as a dormitory for only a few years and then was turned over to the City of Mackinac Island and became the local school. For nearly 150 years the island's students did their ABCs and three Rs there, and daydreamed about adventures they would have when school was out. Additions were built over the years, but the core structure remained intact.

In the 1960s, when a new school was built on the Borough Lot below Grand Hotel, the Park Commission purchased the Indian Dormitory, restored it and installed a museum. The basement and first floor were furnished as they would have been in the 1840s, and the upstairs served to display Indian artifacts arranged on themes derived from Henry W. Longfellow's epic poem, "The Song of Hiawatha."

Since the Park Commission's collection of Indian artifacts was limited, most of the items were on loan from the extensive private collection of Richard Pohrt. Eventually, the borrowed items were returned and replaced with other artifacts acquired by purchase or gift.

The Indian Dormitory was the first building restoration undertaken directly by the staff of the Mackinac Island State Park Commission, and it served as a model for work that would come later.

Restoration was finally carried out during the 1980s on the 1829 Mission Church, which the Park Commission had acquired in 1955. Since it was not a revenue-producing building, revenue-bond proceeds could not be spent on it, and for many years the commission merely maintained it. Later, funds were provided through Federal historic-preservation programs and a significant fund-raising effort by the volunteer state park support organization, Mackinac Associates. The Associates raised more than $20,000 for the project by "selling" pews to donors.

Keith R. Widder, the State Park's Curator of History, provided historical research for the Mission Church project, and later based his doctoral dissertation at Michigan State University on his research on the Mackinac Mission.

The restoration was a major project. At one point, the entire structure was wrapped in a tent so it could be fumigated to eliminate powder post beetles. The church basement and belfry needed considerable repair, and once the structural work was finished, paint chips from the interior were analyzed to determine the original colors. Now restored, the church is open daily and is a popular venue for summer weddings.

BEYOND THE FORT

RIGHT: The Benjamin Blacksmith Shop in its original condition.

ONE OF THE MOST INTERESTING old buildings the Park Commission has restored is the island blacksmith's shop. The commission acquired the shop—and all its contents—in the late 1960s from the family of Herbert Benjamin, the island's smith since the turn of the century. There was one proviso: The shop building had to be removed from its site at the western end of Market Street.

The commission accepted the offer, and found a new site on the east part of the Biddle House lot. But before the building could be moved, the park's experts had to photograph and document the contents as Benjamin had left them so the shop could be re-created on its new site. Doing so required hardy dedication, since it was midwinter. The temperature stood at 10 below zero when Assistant Director David Armour and Staff Archaeologist Lyle M. Stone went to work in the unheated shop.

It was no quick and easy task. Mr. Benjamin had never thrown out a thing, on the theory that whatever it was, he might be able to use it sometime. The shop was piled full of all kinds of tools, materials, scrap and unidentifiable whatnot. Armour and Stone assigned designations to each area of the shop, and listed and photographed it all. Later that winter, other park staff removed all the shop's contents.

The new site was smaller than the original, so only about two thirds of the blacksmith shop could be reconstructed. Floorboards, windows and other pieces were salvaged and used in the reconstruction, and all the objects were put back in appropriate places.

Since opening in 1970 the restored Blacksmith Shop has been a working exhibit. Skilled smiths use the tools to reproduce ironwork for other building restorations and make some items for sale. Interpretation has always been the primary function.

In 1985 the park's blacksmith, Dennis Bradley, invited other blacksmiths to a weekend convention on the island, and the response was so enthusiastic that it has become an annual event. Each year, during the course of the weekend, the visiting smiths undertake a special project. One year they made the fish weather vane for the roof of the Officers' Stone Quarters. Another time, they worked on the iron fence in front of the Blacksmith Shop.

Another historic structure that has been restored on a new site is the William McGulpin House, a late 18th-century log house with distinctive French features. The house had seen several additions, but the original log structure remained intact. Architects and historians had studied the building to gather information for the reconstruction of the Priest's house at Michilimackinac, so its age and significance were recognized.

When the Park Commission acquired it in 1982, it was on a lot behind Ste. Anne's Church, and again the gift was on condition that the house be moved. The commission found a new site on a vacant lot at Market and Fort Streets, opposite the Beaumont Memorial.

All the additions were removed and only the log portion was moved. Carpenters replaced the seriously deteriorated rear wall to stabilize the

RIGHT: Moving the McGulpin House

BELOW RIGHT: Restored Biddle House.

building for moving. A house mover then drove the building to its new site. The building was restored with the help of the Mackinac Associates volunteers. It now interprets the early log architecture of Mackinac Island.

The largest historic building which the Park Commission has acquired is the 1825 Mission House. Originally, it contained classrooms, a student dormitory and staff apartments for the Indian mission school of the American Board of Commissioners for Foreign Missions. After the mission closed in the late 1830s, the building was purchased by the Franks family, which managed it as the island's first hotel. They made space for more rooms by raising the roof, but left the building's essential fabric as it was.

By the 1970s, the Mission House was so seriously rotted it was near collapse. The building was surrounded by conference facilities built in the 1950s by Moral Re-Armament and sold in 1970 to the Rev. Rex Humbard, a television evangelist. By 1977 Humbard had his property for sale, and the Park Commission offered to take the crumbling Mission House off his hands for $1.

The commission acquired the building and a small parcel of land around it, and park carpenters immediately went to work to stabilize the structure. The building still is not fully restored, however, although the Park Commission has

spent more than $250,000 on it as money has become available. The initial concept was to turn some of the ground-floor rooms into a museum, but the building now is used entirely for much-needed staff housing.

One of the most significant things about the Mission House, as far as the Mackinac Island State Park Commission is concerned, dates from its very beginnings. The Indian mission school for which it was originally built was directed by the Rev. William Ferry. In the building, his wife, Amanda, gave birth to a son, Thomas W. Ferry. Many years later Thomas W. Ferry served as the first chairman of the Mackinac Island State Park Commission.

18 Friends of the Park

THERE ARE MORE GOOD IDEAS for historical and park development than there is money to pay for them, and the quest for funds is one of the recurring themes in the Mackinac Island State Park Commission's history. In recent years, the commission has found two interesting new sources of funds.

One of those sources is simply a group of friendly neighbors. Various individuals had donated land, historical artifacts, or funds for special State Park projects here and there, but nothing like an ongoing support group had ever been formed, and the commission has always depended mainly on state funds or admissions fees.

So it was perhaps understandable that the Park Commission was a bit leery when, in the late 1970s, Mackinac Island cottagers began talking about forming a private organization to help support State Park programs. The commission was worried that the cottagers were trying to create a rival policy-setting group.

Finally in 1980, after reassurances that such was not the case, the commission gave its blessing, and "Mackinac Associates," came into being. With a board composed of prominent citizens, the Associates function as an independent, non-profit, support organization. Its administrative agent is the Director of the Park Commission, assuring a close link between the Associates and the Commission. Mackinac Associates held its first official event in the Summer of 1981.

More than 1,000 people are now members of the Mackinac Associates, helping broaden the public impact of the commission. In their first 15 years, Mackinac Associates have provided more than $200,000 in donations for numerous park projects and programs.

In return for their fund-raising campaigns and events, members get unlimited free admissions to the Park Commission's historic sites, discounts in the museum shops, and invitations to special behind-the-scenes events. They also get opportunities for volunteer service and the knowledge that their gifts and support help make possible the programs of the Park Commission.

A traditional highlight of the Mackinac Associates' season is the annual G. Mennen Williams "Mackinac Celebration," honoring the memory of the governor who was the driving force behind creation of the commission's historical development programs.

The Associates have also created an Education Endowment Fund to provide ongoing support to the Commission's Education Outreach programs. Under this program, beginning in the late 1980s, park interpretive staff have provided educational programs each winter in Michigan schools. Initially focused on schools within 65 miles of Mackinac, the program now covers the state, and has been expanded to include natural history programs as well as historical presentations.

The other interesting, outside source of support is wallpaper. Right: wallpaper.

The Commission has developed an ongoing partnership with wallpaper and fabric designer Kate Williams, a granddaughter of Louis P. Simon,

BELOW:
Educational outreach programs take the Mackinac story to schools throughout Michigan.

a commissioner in the 1930s and 1940s. She had worked for the State Park during her college years, and after graduation moved to New York City and became a commercial designer. With fond memories of Mackinac experiences still strong, she approached the commission in 1984 with the idea of collaborating on a line of coordinated wallpaper and fabric designs.

Williams developed a number of designs, called the Mackinac Collection and based on Mackinac themes, and licensed them to Waverly/Schumacher, one of the nation's most prestigious manufacturers and distributors of wallpaper and fabric.

The company was delighted with the line. In 1986 it came to Mackinac to shoot photographs for its catalog and promotional materials. The company paid to refurbish Cottage No. 1 and donated $30,000 for furniture for the house, covered with the fabrics.

A stunning catalog resulted in a beautiful article in *House Beautiful* magazine, and the collection was a smashing success in the showrooms. It proved to be Waverly/Schumacher's best-selling line, and when the initial contract expired, they eagerly renewed it. Although sales have diminished from the early days of the project, small royalty checks continue to come in, and over the years the effort has provided thousands of dollars in support of the commission's historic projects.

19 A Slice of History

The Grand Hotel was the impetus to create a golf course on the old fort pasture.

GOLF GOES BACK A LONG WAY on Mackinac, but there were times when the island talked a better game than it played. Getting 18 holes together in one place was harder than teeing off into a strong wind off the Straits, and it took almost a century.

The island's oldest course is Wawashkamo Golf Club, established in 1900 by a group of cottagers on the farm of Peter Early in the center of the island. Laid out as a Scottish "links" course on the site of the 1814 battlefield, it has remained virtually unchanged for almost a century, and its club house still serves as the center for golfing and club activities. Wawashkamo is the oldest,

continuously-played, nine-hole course in Michigan. Built on land now owned by the state, it is still operated by a private club but is open to the public.

About the time Wawashkamo was built, Grand Hotel's owners expressed interest in creating a golf course of their own adjacent to the hotel, and approached the commission in 1901 about using the fort pasture lands. The commission granted the Grand a five-year lease at $100 a year, but the five years passed without a course's being built. In retrospect, it seems likely that the hotel leased the land to keep the commission from leasing it to another developer.

In 1915 the hotel was back and asking (this time through the mayor) for another lease. Again the commission authorized a lease, and again nothing came of it. Finally, two years later in 1917, Grand Hotel leased the land—for ten years at $150 a year, later cut to $50—and built a nine-hole golf course.

Golf grew in popularity in the 1920s, and in 1927, a few years after the State Park bought the Peter Early farm from Early's heirs, the Park Commission developed a plan to expand the nine-hole Wawashkamo course to 18 holes. It turned out to be just another failed golf project.

The plan meant closing a portion of British Landing Road. To maintain a route to British Landing, park authorities built a new road, State Road, in 1927, and justified it as a firebreak, in accordance with a master forestry plan developed in 1914. Along with the new golf course, the commission planned additional cottage sites along the east side of the golf course.

The first hazard that got in the way of the $10,000 project was a lawsuit filed by the City of Mackinac Island, which objected to closing British Landing Road. That delayed things long enough for the Twenties to give way to the Depression, when reductions in state funds made the entire project unaffordable.

An even more ambitious plan to expand the Grand Hotel course met a similar fate during the Depression. The idea was to add nine new holes, on state land northeast of the course the Grand had built on the old Fort pasture. The Park Commission was open to cooperating on this $45,000 project, because commissioners felt it would attract visitors to Mackinac Island in the dark days of the Depression. Some $5,000 of welfare work was used to start clearing the land, funds everyone concerned thought would easily be recouped through greens fees. There was even some optimistic talk that the course might be cut all the way to link up with Wawashkamo, creating a 36-hole-course if the latter were ever expanded. By 1939, an extensive tract had been cleared for the project.

Then came World War II, and the project died. The land was eventually reforested. During the war, times were so hard on Mackinac that the Park Commission reduced the annual rent on the Grand and Wawashkamo golf course lands to $1 each in 1942.

Efforts to have a golf course built in St. Ignace were every bit as futile. Land there was given to the commis-sion for a golf course in the 1930s, but no course ever was built, and the property was later given to the Michigan Department of Conservation.

Golf finally came of age on the island during the 1980s, the start of a golden era for the game in Northern Michigan when new courses were springing up all over and entire golf resorts were being built. During the '80s, the Grand Hotel course was completely redesigned and rebuilt, and renamed "The Jewel."

In the 1990s, Grand Hotel bought an additional nine-hole course, named "The Woods," construction of which had already been started on the lands of the Stonecliffe Estate. At last, after almost a century of trying, the hotel and the island had an 18-hole golf course—even if all 18 aren't in the same place.

The Jewel golf course was completely renovated in 1987.

20 Island Winters

Cross-country skiing has become a major attraction for winter visitors.

UNTIL RECENT YEARS, winter was when Mackinac Island residents took their home back from visitors, and the Park Commission pared its big summer-time staff to a cadre of year-rounders.

There was still work to be done, of course. In the early years of the century, park crews spent winters cutting lumber from windfall trees for use in summer construction projects. Park crews harvested ice from the harbor well into the 1950s, hauling it up to an ice house in the fort for use in ice boxes during the summer. Prior to 1949 the harvest was done in conjunction with Grand Hotel, but when the hotel bought a new ice machine, the park had to go it alone.

By 1947 the park had a snow plow truck and kept the island's roads open so the fire truck could reach any building if need be. Winter was also a time for a limited amount of construction and building maintenance as time and money permitted. But by and large, winter was down time on Mackinac.

In recent years, that has begun to change. The introduction of snowmobiles in the 1960s made crossing to and from the mainland less problematical. Each year, once the "ice bridge" forms, islanders mark a safe route to St. Ignace with discarded Christmas trees. Islanders who used to cross only when essential, by ski or dog sled, now come and go almost routinely. So do snowmobiling visitors to the island. The new airport built in 1965 has made air taxi service to St. Ignace more dependable as well.

Since the 1980s, increasing numbers of visitors have been coming to Mackinac during the winter. Initially, they were mainly summer workers or cottagers who returned to the island to spend Christmas or celebrate the New Year. When they came, however, they discovered how beautiful Mackinac is when it is blanketed by sparkling, white snow that turns the forests into a fairyland. The island's miles of roads and trails beckoned cross country skiing enthusiasts.

Completion of the new water and sewer systems on the Island in 1984 brought water in winter to many cottages for the first time. A new condominium development built at Stonecliffe was designed for year-round use.

An attempt to develop a downhill ski resort at Stonecliffe in the early 1970s failed, partly because of insufficient snow on the slope and partly because of unreliable winter air connections. Mackinac began to draw a different kind of skier in the 1980s with the rise in popularity of cross-country skiing.

In 1993, when a hotel decided to stay open for the Christmas holidays, the story found its way onto national news wires and TV. The response was so great that others followed. The pace of winter activities on the island increased yet more. Now, several hotels and rooming establishments provide year-round accommodations, and a few restaurants remain open in winter.

The State Park has responded to increased use of the park in winter by opening the Visitor's Center during the Christmas holidays, grooming trails for cross-county skiing, and publishing maps for snowmobilers and skiers.

On the mainland, the Park Commission experimented in 1994 with opening Colonial Michili-

mackinac on two winter weekends, complete with living-history interpretations to demonstrate conditions at the fort during winters two centuries ago. So many visitors showed up that two three-day weekends were scheduled for 1995.

21   Current Events

The elegant Grand Hotel carriage transports guests up the Grand Hill.

BEFORE DR. EUGENE T. PETERSEN retired as park superintendent in 1985, he had been increasingly restless because of changes the State Park Commission had been undergoing after 20 years of relative stability. The changes arose largely out of the vicissitudes of politics. From 1963 to 1983, Michigan's governors were Republicans, first George Romney and then William G. Milliken, who served 13 years—longer than any other governor. Moreover, Milliken generally reappointed commissioners as long as they wished to serve, and Petersen had developed close working relationships with them—especially with Sheldon B. Smith, the chairman from 1975-1983.

Turnover came to the commission in 1983, however, when Democrat James Blanchard took office. He believed in new blood. He named a new chairman, William M. Ellmann, and replaced members as their terms expired. (A notable exception was Kenneth C. Teysen, resident commissioner from Mackinaw City; appointed in 1965, he continues to serve to this day.)

While it may have led indirectly to Petersen's departure, good came of Governor Blanchard's appointing close associates to the commission. In so doing, Blanchard forged new, close ties between the commission and the state's executive office. This alliance, coupled with a legislature in Democratic hands, meant fresh funds for commission programs.

Among the beneficiaries of these funds were the park's buildings on Mackinac Island. In 1985, when the island was again to be the site of the Midwest Governors' Conference, the state sup-

plied the Park Commission with $600,000 for renovations, roof repair and repainting of "Michigan's Crown Jewel." By using Mackinac Island for many meetings and conferences, Blanchard helped bring new prominence and stature to the Park Commission.

When Dr. Petersen stepped down, his assistant, Dr. David A. Armour, served as acting superintendent until the commission named a successor early in 1986. The new director, David L. Pamperin, came from the Manitowoc Maritime Museum, and brought a professional background in museum operations.

Building on program foundations laid by Dr. Petersen, Pamperin set out to increase the commission's earned income and grant revenue. The former was especially difficult during a time when historic sites all over the country were suffering declining attendance. The Park Commission was feeling the trend; although Fort Mackinac held its own, attendance at the mainland sites had declined.

Pamperin added public relations and marketing staff and undertook a program to build the parks' image and identity. The Park Commission renamed the system of parks as "Mackinac State Historic Parks," comprising four parks, each with its own identity. "Fort Mackinac" was separated from "Mackinac Island State Park," Old Mill Creek became simply "Mill Creek," and Fort Michilimackinac was renamed "Colonial Michilimackinac."

To augment income for continuing expansion of historical programs, Pamperin expanded the museum shops, which until then had mainly sold only the commission's own publications. Each of the enlarged shops carries only items which reflect the educational mission of its particular park, and takes great care to avoid competing with local businesses.

Pamperin also provided clear direction for future park programs, undertaking a planning effort with the support of a grant from the National Endowment for the Humanities. This led to a 10-year plan for the 1990s which identified new programs and staff additions required for them. The plan also identified some exhibitions created in the 1960s which needed to be replaced, and pointed to a need for greater care of the Park Commission's collections of historic objects to conform to current professional standards.

As part of this long-range planning process, the Park Commission developed a new mission statement:

> The mission of Mackinac State Historic Parks is to enable present and future generations to understand, appreciate and support the historical and aesthetic significance of the Straits of Mackinac. To accomplish this mission of stewardship, Mackinac State Historic Parks will collect, preserve, study and interpret the unique cultural and natural resources of this region. These responsibilities will be carried out in accordance with the highest professional standards for the benefit, enjoyment and education of the public.

A new, 6,000-square-foot Heritage Center was constructed in the service area on Mackinac Island, to provide a home for the growing col-

lection of historic objects and records. It represents the state of the art, with precise temperature and humidity controls and other protective systems. Most artifacts and documents not on display are kept in this building, where they receive professional care and are available for research. The commission added the post of Curator of Collection to oversee the Heritage Center, and hired a professional preparator to maintain exhibits and produce new displays.

These additions marked a significant maturation of the Park Commission staff. In the Petersen era, when staff was limited, each person wore many hats, changing them as situations required. They were generalists, applying their several skills to changing, seasonal work loads. In the late 1980s, as the parks' historical programs matured, more specialists came on board, each devoting full energy to a single function.

RIGHT: St. Anne's Catholic Cemetery.

Rollerblader on
M-185.

This shift was reflected in a spate of new job titles—Curator of History, Curator of Collections, Conservator, and Curator of Interpretation.

There were shifts in staff emphasis as well. As restoration of Fort Mackinac approached completion, for instance, construction work lessened and retiring carpenters were not replaced. In some specialties, the commission began to rely more on staff and less on "regular contractors."

One museum project in St. Ignace, in which Governor James Blanchard took interest, consumed a great deal of staff time in the late 1980s but came to naught. It was to have been a transportation museum, and funds for planning and research were made available through James Pitz, Director of the Michigan Department of Transportation (MDOT). In 1987, an analysis of tourism in the Straits area by Market Opinion Research concluded that such a facility would attract enough people to be feasible if it had an operating subsidy. MDOT decided to proceed with developing the concept and provided funds through the Mackinac Bridge Authority. A $40,000,000 Transportation Museum was planned and sources of capital funds identified. However, the problem of a continuous operating subsidy was never solved and the project was abandoned.

THE YEAR 1991 BROUGHT change to the Park Commission. Early in the year, a new governor—John Engler—took office and soon appointed several new commissioners. Among them was Dennis O. Cawthorne, Engler's choice for chairman, who holds that position at the Park Commission's centennial.

In May of that year, Director Pamperin resigned to take a position with the Historical Society of Wisconsin. Again, Dr. David A. Armour, as his assistant, became acting director. He served until the commission hired Pamperin's successor the next January.

During this time, Mackinac State Historic Parks hosted scholars from all over North America and Europe at the Sixth International Conference on the History of the Fur Trade. The Park Commission's curator of history, Dr. Keith R. Widder, presided over the conference. Mackinac was the perfect site, since fur had been the foundation of the area's economy for nearly 200 years. Later the Mackinac State Historic Parks and Michigan State University Press jointly published selections from papers presented at the conference.

Pamperin's successor is the present director, Carl R. Nold, who had been director of The State Museum of Pennsylvania. He had been on Mackinac only a few days when he had a controversy to deal with. The issue was lease fees—the rents paid by owners of cottages on state land—and the resulting brouhaha called to mind the earliest days of the State Park.

The fees had been drastically lowered in the Depression in hopes of keeping cottages occupied. Since then, they had not been increased, although real-estate values had risen immensely. By the 1990s, properties purchased for $5,000 in the 1940s had become worth 100 times that, yet lease fees remained at Depression-era levels.

LEFT: A British drummer overlooks Fort Michilimackinac.

BELOW: Map of the Straits of Mackinac. The locations of Mackinac Island State Park, Colonial Michilimackinac and Historic Mill Creek are shown in purple.

Chairman Cawthorne appointed a blue-ribbon citizens' committee to evaluate the fees in light of property values and real estate taxes on comparable property elsewhere in the state. The committee recommended sharp increases. As leases expired, the panel said, yearly rents should increase—to $3,000 on the West Bluff, $2,000 on the East Bluff, and $1,000 for remote locations. They also suggested additional, annual increases based on the rate of inflation. The howls of complaint from cottagers were reminiscent of the situation in 1895, when the first commission doubled rates from $50 to $100. On Mackinac, history tends to repeat itself.

Director Nold survived that early test to develop his interest in high, professional levels of care for the parks' historical collections. Soon after he arrived, the commission adopted stringent research requirements so building preservation and restoration would conform to current professional standards.

Under Nold, a registrar has been added to the staff to oversee computerization of museum records, including data on more than two million artifacts that have been uncovered by the parks' archaeologists. Over the years, maintaining intellectual and physical control of the commission's collections had grown into a formidable task. The artifacts are located at many sites, and the Park Commission's archaeological laboratory and primary storage area are in the commission's administration offices in Lansing. Lansing is also now the site of the parks' main library of books, photos, maps, plans, microfilm, and art. Long range plans call for centralizing these collections

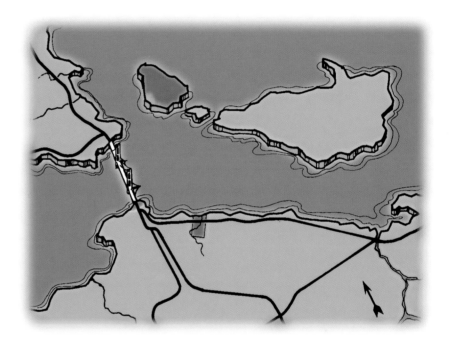

eventually at the Straits.

The Park Commission is ever mindful that part of its mission is to enable people to "understand, appreciate and support" the history and beauty of the Straits, and strives to make its programs available to a wider public. Sign language interpreters are now available for hearing-impaired visitors. Ramps now allow visitors in wheelchairs to visit buildings at Fort Mackinac and Michilimackinac, and to climb the bluff to the nature trails at Mill Creek. Growing numbers of visitors in electric-powered wheelchairs are enjoying visits to the Straits.

New programs have been designed for children and senior citizens, and new winter events make park facilities available at times when they were previously closed. Mackinac Island State

RIGHT: Sunset over Fort Michilimackinac.

FAR RIGHT: The Governor's porch overlooks Fort Mackinac and the town below.

BELOW: Mackinac Island State Park, showing land acquisitions from 1895 to 1995.

Park is for the "benefit, enjoyment and education of the public," and the Park Commission remains committed to that goal.

ALTHOUGH THE PARK Commission deals largely with the past, it has always looked towards the future, mindful of resources it must protect and challenges it must meet.

At the close of the commission's first century, development pressure is increasing on the land resources of the Straits area. The Park Commission must constantly weigh the public good and the need to protect renewable and non-renewable resources. Trees can replace themselves, perhaps, but archaeological treasures, once destroyed, are gone forever. Park lands converted to other uses are difficult—if not impossible—to regain.

In recent years, a legal mechanism called a "conservation easement," has come into wide use all over the country for preserving precious real estate from future development. Simply put, such easements let property owners retain title to land while giving the development rights to someone else—such as the Park Commission—who will never develop it. The owner gets a tax deduction equal to the reduced value of the property, and the public gets land forever protected from development. The first such easement on Mackinac Island was granted to the commission in

1994 by Grand Hotel, protecting the "sandy beach" area below the hotel.

Surely, the future also holds many more discoveries about Mackinac's past. Many stories remain untold, or even undiscovered in Mackinac's attics, and there are still many historic treasures waiting to be found and shared. Some of the treasure lies far from the Straits; steamer trunks in Virginia and in Sante Fe, New Mexico, have recently yielded Mackinac manuscripts—some of them published in *The Chaplain's Lady* and *A Boy at Fort Mackinac: The Diary of Harold Dunbar Corbusier 1883-1884, 1892*.

Dr. Joseph Peyser, a University of Indiana professor doing research for the Park Commission under contract, was recently in France seeking documents detailing early Mackinac history. He discovered many fascinating items which he is currently translating from French to English for publication.

Mackinac has been described by some as an "island cursed by history," but is has also been blessed by that history, and by natural beauty and charm. From this raw material in 1895, the commission has built a park system one authority—*National Geographic Traveller* magazine—has recognized as one of the nation's ten best state parks.

In 1995 the Mackinac Island State Park Commission looks back in celebration of its first century of stewardship, and ahead to the challenges of another 100 years.

Original Park 1895

1910-1930

1940-1950

1960-1970

Conservation Easement

Formerly owned

CREDITS

Photography Credits:

Mackinac Island State Park Commission: All photographs except as noted below.

Aero-Metric Engineering, Inc.: page 45.

H. J. Bell: page 80.

Doug Elbinger: pages ii, vi, vii.

H. D. Ellis: page 73.

Dietrich Floeter: page 81.

Lenore Goodheart: page 57-bottom.

Grand Hotel: page 44.

Johnson's Studio, Cheboygan: page 70.

Thomas Kachadurian: pages iv, 15, 17-top, 18-bottom, 32-top, 55-both, 79, 83-top, 84-left, 89-top, 91-left, 93-left, 97, 124, 125-both, 126, 127.

Balthazar Korab: page 21.

Library of Congress: pages 11, 12 top, 20, 23-bottom.

Michigan Department of Conservation: pages 56, 62-both.

Michigan Historical Commission: page 24

Milwaukee Public Museum: page 38-left.

Photair/Ted Cline: pages 9, 53.

William and Lornie Porter: page 63.

Dave Richards: page 123.

State of Michigan Archives: pages 8, 57-top

Agnes Shine: page 16.

West Michigan Tourist Association: page 37.

The Author Wishes to Acknowledge:

Carolyn Artman	R. Daniel Musser III
Lee Barnett	Victor Nelhiebel
Roger Boettcher	Carl R. Nold
Graydon DeCamp	Eugene T. Petersen
William Fritz	Phil Porter
Dale Gallagher	State of Michigan Archives
John Gram	Kay Stemkoski
Grand Hotel	Lorna Straus
Thomas Kachadurian	Keith R. Widder
R. Daniel Musser Jr.	

BIBLIOGRAPHY

Manuscript Material

Mackinac Island State Park Commission

Minutes of Meetings, 1895-1995, 15 Vols.
Superintendents' Reports and Correspondence, 1907-1983
Superintendents' Letterbook, 1896-1902
Samuel Poole, Superintendent Correspondence, 1894-1901
George Bates Truscott Scrapbook, ca. 1860-1952
Oral History Transcripts

Bailey, Robert Matthew	1973
Bogan, James Joseph	1973
Davey, Joseph F.	1982
Gallagher, Dale	1994
Lang, Otto W.	1975
Pero, Morton H.	1973
Pfeiffleman, Herbert Eugene	1974
Puttkammer, Ernst Wilfred	1973
Shine, Agnes	1973
Truscott, Philip Keast	1973

Photograph Collections
Map and Plan Collections

State Archives of Michigan

Agency Papers	
Administration	1949-1965
Attorney General	1895-1966
Auditor General	1933-34, 1942-52, 1955-58
Conservation	1833-1961
Executive	1895-1912, 1914-15, 1923-30
	1943-48, 1957-60, 1966-67
Historical Commission	1954-1959
Natural Resources	1930-1984

Personal Papers
    Adams, Ira A.
    Andrews, Roger M.

Publications of the Mackinac Island State Park Commission

General

Armour, David A.
    Fort Michilimackinac Sketchbook. 1975.
    Soldiers of Mackinac. 1975.
    Editor, *Treason? At Michilimackinac: The Proceedings of a General Court Martial held in Montreal in October, 1768, for the Trial of Major Robert Rogers.* 1967.
    Editor, *Massacre at Mackinac: Alexander Henry's Travels and Adventures in Canada and the Indian Territories between the Years 1760 and 1764.* 1966. Retitled *Attack at Michilimackinac.* 1971.
Armour, David A., and Keith R. Widder
    At the Crossroads: Michilimackinac During the American Revolution. 1978.

Michilimackinac: A Handbook to the Site. 1980, Revised edition 1990.

Brown, Jennifer S.H., W. J. Eccles and Donald P. Heldman, Editors.
The Fur Trade Revisited: Selected Papers of the Sixth North American Fur Trade Conference, Mackinac Island, Michigan, 1991. Jointly published with Michigan State University Press. 1994.

Gringhuis, Dirk
The Lore of the Great Turtle: Indian Legends of Mackinac Retold. 1970.
Were-Wolves and Will-O-the-Wisps: French Tales of Mackinac Retold. 1974.
The Young Voyageur. 1969.

Kelton, Dwight H.
Annals of Fort Mackinac. Chicago. 1882. Reprinted, 1992. ·

Mackinac Island State Park Commission
British Landing Nature Area Checklist. 1993.
Historic Mackinac Island Visitor's Guide. 1994.
Mackinac Island Bird Checklist. 1991.
Mackinac Island State Park, Mackinac Island, Michigan: Report of the Board of Commissioners, January 19, 1909.
Mackinac Island Visitor's Guide. 1992.
Mill Creek Wildlife Checklist. 1991.
1937-1938 Report of the Mackinac Island State Park Commission of Michigan State Parks at Mackinac Island and Mackinaw City. 1938.
1933 and 1934 Report of the Mackinac Island State Park Commission.

May, George S.
The Forts of Mackinac. 1962.
Historic Guidebook Mackinac Island. 1962.
War 1812. 1962.
Editor, *The Doctor's Secret Journal.* 1960.

Nicholas, Edward
The Chaplain's Lady: Life and Love at Fort Mackinac. 1987.

Petersen, Eugene T.
France at Mackinac: A Pictorial Record of French Life and Culture, 1715-1760. 1968.
Gentlemen on the Frontier: A Pictorial Record of the Culture of Michilimackinac. 1964.
Guide Book for Mackinac Island Visitors. 1979.
Mackinac and the Porcelain City. 1985.
Mackinac Island: Its History in Pictures. 1973.
Michilimackinac: Its History and Restoration. 1962, Revised edition, 1968.

Porter, Phil
The Wonder of Mackinac: A Guide to the Natural History of Mackinac Island. 1984.
Editor, *A Boy at Fort Mackinac: The Diary of Harold Dunbar Corbusier, 1883-84, 1892.* 1994.

Stone, Lyle M.
Archaeological Site Survey in the Mackinac Straits. 1975.
Fort Michilimackinac, 1715-1781: An Archaeological Perspective on the Revolutionary Frontier. Jointly published with Michigan State University, Publications of the Museum, Anthropological Series, Vol. 2. 1974.

Widder, Keith R.
Dr. William Beaumont: The Mackinac Years. 1975.
Reveille Till Taps: Soldier Life at Fort Mackinac, 1780-1895. 1972.

Reports in Mackinac History and Archaeology

1. Stone, Lyle M.
Archaeological Investigation of the Marquette Mission Site, St. Ignace, Michigan, 1971: A Preliminary Report. 1972.
2. Petersen, Eugene T.
The Preservation of History at Mackinac. 1972.
3. Dunnigan, Brian Leigh
King's Men at Mackinac: The British Garrisons, 1780-1796. 1973.
4. Widder, Keith R.
Mackinac National Park, 1875-1895. 1975.
5. Hamilton, T. M.
Firearms on the Frontier: Guns at Fort Michilimackinac, 1715-1781. 1976.
6. Heldman, Donald P. and William L. Minnerly
The Powder Magazine at Fort Michilimackinac: Excavation Report. 1977.
7. Dunnigan, Brian Leigh
The British Army at Mackinac, 1812-1815. 1980.
8. Porter, Phil
View from the Veranda: The History and Architecture of the Summer Cottages on Mackinac Island. 1981.
9. Petersen, Eugene T.
Mackinac in Restoration. 1983.
10. Dunnigan, Brian Leigh
Fort Holmes. 1984.
11. Porter, Phil
The Eagle at Mackinac: The Establishment of United States Military and Civil Authority on Mackinac Island, 1796-1802. 1991.

Archaeological Completion Report Series

1. Heldman, Donald P.
Excavations at Fort Michilimackinac, 1976: The Southeast and South Southeast Row Houses. 1977.
2. Heldman, Donald P.
Excavations at Fort Michilimackinac, 1977: House One of the South Southeast Row House. 1978.
3. Heldman, Donald P., and Robert T. Grange, Jr.
Excavations at Fort Michilimackinac: 1978-1979, The Rue de la Babillarde. 1981.
4. Williams, J. Mark, and Gary Shapiro
A Search for the Eighteenth Century Village at Michilimackinac: A Soil Resistivity Survey. 1982.
5. Hauser, Judith Ann
Jesuit Rings from Fort Michilimackinac and Other European Contact Sites. 1982.
6. Heldman, Donald P.
Archaeological Investigations at French Farm Lake in Northern Michigan, 1981-82: A British Colonial Farm Site. 1983.
7. Frurip, David J., Russell Malewicki and Donald P. Heldman
Colonial Nails from Michilimackinac: Differentiation by Chemical

BIBLIOGRAPHY

and Statistical Analysis. 1983.

8. Prahl, Earl J., and Mark Branstner
Archaeological Investigations on Mackinac Island, 1983: The Watermain and Sewer Project. 1984.

9. Scott, Elizabeth M.
French Subsistence at Fort Michilimackinac, 1715-1781: The Clergy and the Traders. 1985.

10. Martin, Patrick Edward
The Mill Creek Site and Pattern Recognition in Historical Archaeology. 1985.

11. Halchin, Jill Y.
Excavations at Fort Michilimackinac, 1983-1985: House C of the Southeast Row House, The Solomon-Levy-Parant House. 1985.

12. Grange, Roger T., Jr.
Excavations at Fort Mackinac, 1980-1982: The Provision Storehouse. 1987.

13. Hamilton, T. M., and K. O. Emery
Eighteenth-Century Gunflints from Fort Michilimackinac and other Colonial Sites. 1988.

14. Adams, Diane L.
Lead Seals from Fort Michilimackinac, 1715-1781. 1989.

15. Morand, Lynn L.
Craft Industries at Fort Michilimackinac, 1715-1781. 1994.

Mackinac History, Volume I

1. Petersen, Eugene T.
Clay Pipes: A Footnote to Mackinac's History. 1963.

2. May, George S.
The Askin Inventory: A Mackinac Businessman's Property in 1778. 1963

3. Mackinac Island State Park Commission
Mackinac Island Tourist Map. 1964.

4. Petersen, Eugene T.
Wilkes and Liberty. 1964.

5. May, George S.
The Mess at Mackinac Or, No More Sagamity for Me, Thank You! 1964.

6. May, George S.
The Reconstruction of the Church of Ste. Anne de Michilimackinac. 1964.

7. Campbell, J. Duncan
Military Buttons: Long Lost Heralds of Fort Mackinac's Past. 1965.

8. Armour, David A.
Made in Mackinac: Crafts at Fort Michilimackinac. 1966.

9. Stone, Lyle M.
Archaeology at Fort Michilimackinac. 1967.

10. Armour, David A.
The Women of Michilimackinac. 1967.

11. May, George S.
John C. Pemberton: A Pennsylvania Confederate at Fort Mackinac. 1968.

12. Gringhuis, Dirk
In Grey-White and Blue: French Troops at Fort Michilimackinac, 1715-1760. 1969.

Mackinac History, Volume II

1. Gringhuis, Dirk
Indian Costume at Mackinac: Seventeenth and Eighteenth Century. 1972.

2. Widder, Keith R.
Justice at Mackinac: The Execution of Private James Brown. 1974.

3. Dunnigan, Brian Leigh
Milestones of the Past: Military Buttons and Insignia from Mackinac. 1975.

4. Davis, James S.
Mackinac Island Scout Service Camp. 1975.

5. Gerin-Lajoie, Marie
Translator, *Fort Michilimackinac in 1749: Lothiniere's Plan and Description.* 1976.

6. Armour, David A.
David and Elizabeth: The Mitchell Family of the Straits of Mackinac. 1982.

Other References

Andrews, Roger M.
Old Fort Mackinac on the Hill of History. Menominee, Michigan. 1938.

Bailey, John R.
Mackinac, Formerly Michilimackinac: A History and Guide Book with Maps. 6th edition. Grand Rapids, Michigan. 1909. First published 1895.

Brose, David S.
The Custer Road Dump Site: An Exercise in Victorian Archaeology. *Michigan Archaeologist*, Vol.13, No.2, June, 1967.

Brown, Margaret K.
"Glass from Fort Michilimackinac: A classification for Eighteenth Century Glass," *Michigan* Vol. 17, Nos 3-4, September - December 1971.

Dunnigan, James P.
Around My World in Eighty Years. Privately printed. December, 1990.

Emery, Benjamin Franklin
Fort Holmes. Detroit. 1931.
Fort Michilimackinac, 1715-1780: The Scene of the Pontiac Massacre, June 4, 1763. Detroit. 1931.

McKee, Russell
Mackinac: The Gathering Place. Lansing, Michigan. 1981.

Maxwell, Moreau S. and Lewis H. Binford
Excavation at Fort Michilimackinac, Mackinac City, Michigan, 1959 Season. Michigan State University, Publications of the Museum, Cultural Series, Vol. 1, No. 1. East Lansing, Michigan. 1961.

Michigan Historical Commission
Lewis Cass Day on Mackinac Island, August 28, 1915. Michigan Historical Commission, Bulletin No. 7. Lansing, Michigan. 1916.
Nicolet Day on Mackinac Island. Michigan Historical Commission, Bulletin No. 6. Lansing, Michigan. 1916.

Miller, J. Jefferson, II, and Lyle M. Stone
Eighteenth-Century Ceramics from Fort Michilimackinac: A Study in

Historical Archaeology. Washington, D.C.: Smithsonian Institution Press. 1970.

O'Brien, Frank A.
Names of Places of Interest on Mackinac Island, Michigan. Michigan Historical Commission,Bulletin No.5. Lansing, Michigan. 1916.

Petersen, Eugene T.
Inside Mackinac. St. Ignace, Michigan. 1990.

Piljac, Pamela A. and Thomas M. Piljac
Mackinac Island: Historic Frontier, Vacation Resort, Timeless Wonderland. Portage, Indiana. 1988.

Ranville, Judy, and Nancy Campbell
Memories of Mackinaw. Petoskey, Michigan. 1976.

Rinehart, Charles J.
Crucifixes and medallions: their role at Fort Michilimackinac. Columbia, S. C. 1990

Stanley, George M.
Pre-Historic Mackinac Island. Michigan Department of Conservation, Geological Survey Division, Publication 43, Geological Series 36. Lansing, Michigan. 1945.

Summerfield, Mary Duffina
The Voice of the Turtle: A Pictorial Narrative of Early Mackinac Island, Formerly Michilimackinac. Grand Marais, Michigan. 1975.

Wickman, G. H.
Mackinac under Three Flags. Fifth Edition. Menominee, Michigan. 1946.

Williams, Meade C.
Early Mackinac: A Sketch Historical and Descriptive. 1897/1901/1912. Reprinted with an Introductory Essay by Larry Massie. Au Train, Michigan. 1987.

Wood, Edwin O.
Historic Mackinac: The Historical, Picturesque and Legendary Features of the Mackinac Country. 2 Vols. New York. 1918.

INDEX

INDEX